I0811524

Blood Saga

Dissecting the Cult Film Repo! The Genetic Opera

Blood Saga

Dissecting the Cult Film Repo! The Genetic Opera

Staci Wilson

1984

DISSECTING THE CULT FILM REPO! THE GENETIC OPERA

Copyright © 2024 by Staci Wilson

All rights reserved. No portion of this book may be used or reproduced without prior written permission, except in the case of brief quotations embodied in critical articles and reviews.

This is a work of nonfiction. The events and experiences detailed herein have been faithfully rendered as remembered by the author and interviewees, to the best of their ability. Except where noted, quotations were obtained directly by the author.

Repo! The Genetic Opera is © 2008 Lionsgate Films

COVER DESIGN: Hag Cult
LAYOUT: Arkadii Pankevich
EDITOR: Amy Bee

Image credits appear in the back of the book.

Library of Congress Cataloging-in-Publication Data has been applied for.

ISBNs: 9781948221337 (softbound), 9781948221344 (ebook)

1984 Publishing logo is © and ™ of 1984 Publishing, LLC.

Printed in USA.

1984 PUBLISHING
Cleveland, Ohio / USA
1984Publishing.com
info@1984publishing.com

FIRST EDITION / FIRST PRINTING

This book is for Shem Andre Byron,
a true champion of *Repo! The Genetic Opera*
(and who is probably still singing its praises in the afterlife!).

CONTENTS

INTRODUCTION

On November 7, 2008, a little-known but ambitious rock opera feature film opened on eight screens in five US cities (Austin, New York, Los Angeles, Las Vegas, and San Francisco), grossing $53,684 over its first few days. Not too shabby for an indie, but considering the director's previous film brought in $33.6 million on its opening weekend, the rock opera was a bona fide box office bomb.

The above-referenced film is *Repo! The Genetic Opera.* (Henceforth referred to as *Repo.*) Despite its rocky start, *Repo* has developed into a cult classic, commanding a *Rocky Horror*-like fanbase. This is a great clapback to film critic Frank Scheck of the *Hollywood Reporter,* who wrote in his initial review: "This would-be cult film is unlikely to inspire *Rocky Horror*-like devotion." To this day, shadow casts (recreating the action to a live audience while the movie plays behind them) continue to sing and dance in time to *Repo.*

How did *Repo* become an underground sensation? And what's my connection to this cult classic?

We'll dive into the whys and hows in the following chapters, but first, I ask that you use your imagination: What if *The*

Big Lebowski-era Coen Brothers had helmed *Blade Runner*? Isn't that something you'd want to see? That you'd *pay* to see?

After seeing an early press screening, my first jotted note was: "Orwell's *1984* meets *Cemetery Man*." Then I thought, "No, it's more *Brazil* vs. *The Rocky Horror Picture Show*." However, it could be *Gattaca* gets with *Sweeney Todd*. Or maybe even *Moulin Rouge!* melded with *Fahrenheit 451*. Then again, there's a little *The Wizard of Oz* in there. And some *Metropolis*. See what I mean? This outlandish, lavish tale is impossible to pigeonhole—a quality that I love, even as it gives studios, marketing people, and publicists nervous tics—but what it really has going for it is heart. And *hearts*.

Repo is set in a not-too-distant future where it will be fashionable to not only clothe and accessorize yourself with designer brands, but it'll be trés trendy to be super chic from the inside out. As you pass through the ever-present X-ray machines, everyone will see your Gucci guts, Halston heart, and Prada pancreas. But what happens when you can't make your payments? Much like a leased vehicle subject to repossession, so too are these impressive innards. When the singing, slaying Repo Man comes to collect, there's no escape!

The movie boasts an all-star cast, including Broadway's best gal Sarah Brightman, socialite Paris Hilton, Anthony Stewart Head of *Buffy the Vampire Slayer*, the late Paul Sorvino of *Goodfellas*, Alexa PenaVega of the *Spy Kids* franchise, Bill Moseley of the *Texas Chainsaw Massacre* franchise, and Skinny Puppy frontman Nivek Ogre (née Kevin Ogilvie) in his first starring role.

Perhaps most surprising to audiences and critics was the director, Darren Lynn Bousman, known only as the "*Saw* movies guy" at the time. Yes, there is his signature blood and gore in *Repo*, but it's presented in the manner of a satirist, not a sadist.

As you read, you will learn that Bousman fought long and hard for the opportunity to make the rock opera film. He was shot down repeatedly, with the studio (Lionsgate) insisting that he instead devote his time to the lucrative *Saw* franchise. He ultimately refused to work on another gore flick until he got his way. Eventually, the studio and the director compromised, and *Saw IV* and *Repo* were shot back-to-back in Canada in 2007.

I was a freelance reporter working mainly for *SYFY WIRE* and *Horror.com* when I was invited to fly from Los Angeles to Toronto to cover both films. The *Saw* movies were old hat to me by then, but as I toured the elaborate set of *Repo* and got the rundown from Bousman and writer-composers Darren Gordon Smith and Terrance Zdunich, I immediately knew: *This is for me.* Even though I'm known for my work in the horror and suspense genres, some of my all-time favorite movies include *Hair*, *The Rocky Horror Picture Show*, *Phantom of the Paradise*, *Moulin Rouge!*, *Tommy*, and *All That Jazz*. So, to discover something as unique as *Repo*, well, I was a fan before I even saw the completed movie.

As a reporter and film critic, I've attended hundreds of press tours, set visits, and red-carpet events. They're all fun in their way, but most are instantly forgotten, and rarely does one connect in any meaningful way with the interviewees. *Repo* was different. I'd interviewed Bousman and Moseley before, but there was something about the alchemy of this project that made us all see each other as kindred spirits. In the years to follow, we often socialized, and I took care to support their other creative endeavors (Moseley as a musician with Buckethead, and Ogre in his "ohGr" persona; Bousman as the creator of the Tension Experience, a celebrated immersive haunt).

That October 2007 set visit led to friendships and partnerships still going strong to this day. In 2011, I decided to try my hand at film directing. My first short, an Edgar Allan Poe dark fantasy called *The Key to Annabelle Lee*, stars Ogre in the lead role. My most recent feature film as a director, *The Second Age of Aquarius*, was cowritten and coproduced by Smith; Smith and I also collaborated on the *Rock & Roll Nightmares* book series.

Before I visited the set, *Repo* was just another of the dozens of flicks I was to cover that year. Now, fifteen years later, the friendships and partnerships formed have led to a whole new career.

But *Repo* didn't just redirect the course of *my* life—as you'll see in the pages that follow, it changed many people's lives for the better—and even saved some.

CHAPTER 1
INCEPTION

Shilo Wallace is a quarantined, genetically-infected teen who seizes her freedom despite her overprotective father's precautions and runs with it—availing herself of a dark, exciting underworld. Even though Shilo is on a medication monitor and is tracked with a holographic GPS, her widowed dad, Nathan Wallace, can't be everywhere at once. He's a medical man by day and a covert organ Repo Man by night, so his dance card is pretty full, leaving his daughter open to temptation.

One night, while visiting her mother's tomb, Shilo encounters the charismatic Grave Robber. As the main supplier of Zydrate—a fictional fluid extracted from the brains of freshly buried corpses and said to have euphoric opiate effects—he knows the city and its inhabitants inside and out. He's the compass of the parable, bracketing the action at the beginning and the end. The singing, dancing, slicing and dicing Grave Robber was originally a side character in the stage production of *Repo*, appearing in a ten-minute segment called

The Necromerchant's Debt. Still, he resonated with audiences, and that's how the humble presentation flowered from two guys acting on a small stage to a full-scale Hollywood ensemble production starring an array of icons.

Those two guys onstage were Darren Gordon Smith and Terrance Zdunich. They met while studying acting at South Coast Repertory and in 1999 formed The Gallery and began writing and performing theatrical rock music in the form of ten-minute operas. They stormed the Los Angeles nightclub and theater scenes as a duo, performing at the Metropolitan, the Gig, Cat Club, Coconut Teaszer, and California Institute for Abnormal Arts. Kris Allen of *Coast* magazine wrote that The Gallery were "operatic pranksters who blur the line between rock, theater, and performance art. They perform witty stories of misfits, outcasts, and other human oddities in sound bites of delirious, decadent musical theater. Throw in a couple of songs about walking through graveyards or folding giant penis greeting cards, and you have the makings of a very visual, very intense, and very witty musical concoction."

Smith, who graduated with a Bachelor of Music from New York University and studied ethnomusicology at Wesleyan University, played music professionally in New York and throughout the East Coast early in his career. He plays several instruments—he even took banjo lessons from Peter Tork of The Monkees!—and before forming The Gallery, performed with various musicians ranging from Sophie B. Hawkins to Elliot

Sharp. For the *Repo* soundtrack, he wrote the instrumental score, arranged and orchestrated the bulk of the film's music, sang, and performed on the following instruments: trumpet, sitar, keyboards, guitar, mandolin, percussion, cello, accordion, clarinet, bass, recorder, harmonica, and glockenspiel. *Keyboard* magazine wrote that Smith "stitches rhythmic fragments together with pointillistic hooks, which lace together through cool, shimmery, brooding textures."

Smith has forever been drawn to the absurd and the unusual. As a kid, he loved listening to jazz 78s with his dad, a musician who collected the vinyl of Louis Armstrong, Miles Davis, and Chet Baker. Smith's mom was also a professional musician, and he tried to get in on the act once. "I got drunk at age two on champagne while my mom was having one of her many classical piano concerts. While she played Bach, I got up dancing the Watusi before hitting my head on the piano and passing out." In addition to music, Smith grew up on film, especially silent movies with stars like Charlie Chaplin and Harold Lloyd, and late-night creature features.

Zdunich graduated from Otis College of Art and Design, and his background in the visual arts led him to work in the animation industry as a storyboard artist for animated films like *Firedog*, the live-action biopic *What We Do is Secret* (about the punk band The Germs), and the Oscar-nominated *Into the Wild*, directed by Sean Penn. In addition to these talents, Zdunich sharpened his songwriting and singing skills. He's been described as "powerful and spooky" by *Los Angeles Weekly* and "strutting the stage with imposing ambiance" by *OC Metro.* He was the lead singer for Caligula, a band that performed at the Whiskey and the Troubadour, as well as other clubs.

Zdunich has always been fascinated by dark, underworldly things and applied them to his art and performances—even the name of his early band. "As a preteen, I remember reading how the Roman tyrant Caligula would practice scary grimaces in a mirror to better strike terror into his subjects," he wrote in his blog in 2013. "At that time in my life, I also remember teachers continuously asking me if something was wrong—presumably because I was reading too much literature on insane despots and because I didn't smile enough—so, like Caligula, I would practice faces, happy faces, in my own imperial bedroom looking glass." He later bestowed one of those grins to the countenance of Grave Robber, who charms just before he harms.

When it came to bringing *Repo*'s world to life and populating it with different characters, the writing duo decided that having a medical tie-in would make the most sense because sometimes there's a fine line between truly necessary surgeries and elective procedures.

"We've read about extreme things. Like, there's a survey called the G-Shot, which is essentially injecting silicone or something into a woman's G-spot so that it is enlarged and irritated," Zdunich said. "I used to teach art classes in Calabasas, and it was kind of in a strip mall. There was what I thought was a spa at the end of the shopping center, within walking distance from where I was teaching kids. But for the most part, it was an in-and-out plastic surgery for these wealthy house moms who would essentially drop the kids off at the nannies or with me and then go next door. I walked by once, and they had balloons up and candies out, and I asked, 'What is going on?' And they were like, 'Oh, it's a Botox party' with a straight face." (Or a slack face, as the case may be.) "I guess on some level, I almost respect it because it was like, we're admitting exactly what we are doing. I would think that would be something on some level you would want to keep on the down-low. But they are hanging balloons and banners. So anyway, I think *Repo* is kind of informed by all those. We enjoy the sickness of it."

The scripts for the ten-minute operas were fluid and ever-changing. But the theme of genetics was always at the forefront, Smith said. "It's the age-old nature versus nurture thing. Shilo feels that she is trapped by her genetics, by the past of her father and her mother, and this blood disease that she believes she has. Can we get beyond what our personal histories are? What are things that are immutable within our genetic structure and what are not? What can we change?"

Repo was performed in Los Angeles and New York to underground acclaim. While some Hollywood types expressed interest in adapting the quirky, audacious sci-fi opera into a film, it took a young and inexperienced visionary film school grad to make it happen.

While Smith and Zdunich came of age near cosmopolitan cities, Darren Lynn Bousman was born and raised in Overland Park, Kansas. At his school, academia and sports were de rigueur, but neither of those interested him; he always knew he wanted to make movies. Quentin Tarantino's opening nights were never missed, and he was mightily encouraged after writing a letter to Darren Aronofsky, who answered with friendly advice. Bousman, like Smith and Zdunich, was a music geek. While he didn't perform in bands and he didn't write musicals, he did love the genre—especially in film. Cult classics of the 1970s, such as *Jesus Christ Superstar*, *The Rocky Horror Picture Show*, and *The Apple* were among his favorites and would later serve as touchstones for *Repo.*

The first step to realizing his dream of becoming a director was completing film school at Full Sail University in Orlando, Florida. He wrote and directed one low-budget feature, *Identity Lost*, then made the big trek to Hollywood. But he had to start at the bottom: literally. One of his first jobs was on the *X-Files* series set, guarding the honey wagon (toilet). Bousman was fired due to constantly working on his screenplay while on the job. That script was called *The Desperate* and was eventually turned into *Saw II*—the film that fast-tracked his career.

When Bousman saw *Repo,* he was blown away by the originality and the artistic sensibilities of Smith and Zdunich. He got the libretto and directed the first fully realized stage play in 2001. Around this time, Bousman was also helming music videos such as "So" by Static-X, but his true ambition was to direct a big, splash-making feature film—preferably of *Repo*.

CHAPTER 2

STAGE PLAY

In the early days of Smith and Zdunich performing as The Gallery, their musical show was a fairly loose, free-form performance with few props. "It was just the two of us telling stories," Smith said. "They were always different stories. One took place in 18th century Vienna, and Terrance had a powdered wig he'd wear. Then we started thinking about doing a story about somebody who is in a graveyard and sees different things happening. He's in the underbelly of society, and he observes the kinds of things that so-called normal people don't necessarily see."

"There were a few things we were resolute about. One of them was we wanted this to be an opera, as opposed to a musical. An opera is where people sing from beginning to end; there's no spoken dialogue. Once you get over the artifice of somebody opening their mouth only to sing, hopefully you forget about it. They're singing, but they are telling a story. Two, we wanted science in our science fiction. We studied opera, and we also studied the scientific aspects of being able to implant organs into people. We talked to surgeons. We read copious amounts of Philip K. Dick. It's an over-the-top, fun, somewhat absurd story, but we wanted it to have elements of truth and a real heart for people to grasp onto."

Zdunich said, "We had bottom-of-the-box ideas that really worked. It was a stage show, but some stuff was pretty extreme. We even decorated the lobby with tanks holding organs, and we had IVs draped around, and glowing fluids in vials. We'd bought some animal body parts online that were plastic-sealed in jars, but they were real guts. Those surrounded the stage, and there was blood spilled on the stage too. This particular venue was pretty extreme; it was essentially a warehouse that we rented. I think some plays and stuff probably had gone on there, but certainly nothing as ambitious as what we were trying. [It was] way below code, and nothing really worked. The guy that ran it was really weird.

"The bathroom was behind the stage, and the only way that [anyone in the audience] could get into the bathroom was to actually go over the stage. And we were serving alcohol and stuff without a liquor license. We're pumping drinks into them, and they've gotta pee. So, at the intermission, you would have a line going across the stage. At one point, intermission was, like, forty-five minutes long, so we kind of worked that into the show—the Repo Man would clear the stage."

Costumer Oriel Collins was in a very early incarnation of the play, and she recalled how improv-heavy it was. At first, in addition to working behind the scenes, she wheeled a cart of gory props onstage and helped with organ repos. After a few performances, her role expanded to that of a Gentern (sort of a nurse). "In character, I arrived early in order to have maximum impact before the show began," she said. "I took off my coat to reveal the full skimpy glory of the costume I'd designed: a white pleather bikini top, wrap miniskirt, and fishnets. And to give it a semblance of a nurse's uniform, I donned a stethoscope and little triangular white cap. I had prepared a medical bag with prescription bottles filled with Tic Tacs and Smarties, a prescription pad, Band-Aids, alcohol wipes, and a fake hypodermic needle. I was ready to mingle. I imagined my veins were pumping with Zydrate. Silly emotions were no more; my voice was a monotone, bored. Smiling was out of the question. To say most people found me creepy would be an understatement. I loved it."

"Our cast was amazing," Smith said. "Stephanie Kane played Shilo, Lateefah Devoe and Natalie Salins both played Blind Mag, and Curt Wilson played Nathan/Repo Man. We lucked out because they were so talented and so committed."

Zdunich said his signature character, Grave Robber, was "kind of doing an overall social commentary. One of the things that he saw in this graveyard was an organ Repo Man, and that particular idea seemed to resonate with the various audiences that we played it to. It started as just kind of a wacky concept, but I think as we started to have it grow, it got bigger than what we could ever really do on stage. And as such, I think we wanted it to be a more visual medium. The film, I think, adds horror, but we talked about how it could be a graphic novel. Something more than just here's a live show that you put on, something that has a bigger visual element. We wanted it bigger than it could ever really be as a play."

When Bousman saw *Repo* the musical play, he knew he had to be a part of it. "I was really impressed," Smith recalled, "because he was just out of film school, but he told us he was made to direct the play *and* make the film. We'd heard that before, people be all excited when they want to get a gig, but right off the bat, he's got all these ideas. One I remember was, he wanted to have somebody pretending to be a patron come in with a cell phone, annoying everybody, and then have a Repo Man come and repossess this person right out of the audience. Or, people will have these genetic barcodes, and we will have some problem with the Jesus freak who thinks it's out of the Book of Revelation that people should never have any kind of barcode on them. So, he had this idea of staging outside all these right-wing Bible Belt people with songs boycotting us."

Backed up by true talent, showman's tactics like these had an underground buzz going in no time. Actor Bill Moseley, who would later star in the *Repo* film, heard about the play from a friend, who took him to "this crazy storefront play on Hollywood Boulevard. I remember this stuff called Zydrate, and just cool science fiction aspects. Honestly, I didn't know what it was, but I liked it!

"Fast forward maybe a year or so later, and I was at a Fangoria convention in San Jose, where I had a Q&A onstage to promote the Rob Zombie movies I'd done." The ballroom was large, so two panels were going on simultaneously, separated by a curtain. When Moseley's talk was over, he could hear somebody in the other half of the ballroom still doing their Q&A. "It turned out to be Darren Bousman. He was talking about a play, describing *Repo* and saying it was his dream project. I even went up to him afterward and said I'd seen the show, so we talked a little bit. He was there, obviously, for *Saw*, but he wanted to talk about *Repo*, and that's how I got my first whiff of it becoming a movie."

J. LaRose, who plays a reporter in *Repo*, was already a longtime friend and collaborator of Bousman's when he saw the stage play. "I met Darren when he was just out of film school on the East Coast, but we remained friends after his trek west. He landed out in L.A. and he was doing this small theater piece, so in support, I flew out and got to see one of the shows. It was terrific! It was new to me, that whole L.A. theater scene: small, underground, black box theater-type stuff. And they had genius music. Darren [Smith] did a great job, and Terrance, and all the people involved. And man, it was pretty great to see it go from there to where it ended up as a film."

Alisa Burket, who plays one of Rotti Largo's Henchgirls in *Repo*, is also one of the few actors familiar with the play before the film went into production. After playing in Los Angeles, *Repo* went to New York, where it played off-off-Broadway at Wings Theater on Christopher Street in extreme West Village. "I was living in New York pursuing acting in the laziest of ways but pursuing it nonetheless. I was going through audition calls on *Backstage.com*, and when I read the description for the show, specific phrases jumped out at me: not your parents' opera, *Rocky Horror* meets *Bladerunner*, rock opera... my interest was piqued.

"I remember it was an open audition, so I wasn't going for any particular role. I just got up there and sang whatever song I had trudged up and did my best to nail the choreography part of the audition. I studied music in college, but I love dancing, so that part was the most fun for me. It was a surprisingly supportive audition process, and I hoped I'd get a part based on that."

Burket thought the guys seemed like they'd be good to work with. "When I got the call that I was cast in the play as a Henchgirl, I was so excited! There were only two of us. We flanked him on both sides and had our choreography down, so we moved at the exact same time as each other. We had fake guns, and we'd use garter belts on our thighs as the holster. I felt so badass. I'm an only child, so growing up, I'd play in my backyard by myself a lot and usually dressed up as some sort of warrior goddess—Athena, Wonder Woman, She-Ra—so this was a bit of a dream come true."

Once the New York troupe started rehearsals, the play became an endeavor of passion and love for most of the actors and crew. "It was low budget," Burket recalled, "so we were all bringing our own stuff in, creating our own costumes, doing our own hair and makeup looks based on direction from Darren [Smith] and Terrance. It was so much fun. We all believed in this play so much, I think in large part because of how much Darren and Terrance were putting into it; that bled through to all of us. If you're a performer, you want to be a part of a creative baby and help it grow, and they allowed us to do that in our own ways. They were so respectful and encouraging of all of us as performers, but they were also very clear with their vision of the play. That's rare, and we recognized that."

Burket and her fellow cast members were given prerecorded music tracks of the songs they'd be performing onstage. "On our first day [of rehearsal], we all pretty much knew the songs by heart already. We all loved the music and singing it so much that even when we weren't in a scene, we would perform it for each other in the back while it was being performed on stage. It never got tiring, even though we performed a lot of daily shows. There was always something new to discover in the music. It just felt so good to sing it, harmonize with it, move with it, and perform it. Pretty sure we were all listening to the soundtrack for fun in our off time. I know I was!"

Although *Repo* was a fan favorite, it wasn't paying anyone's bills. A couple of years after the play's final run, Bousman got his big break directing *Saw II*. The first *Saw* was a smash hit, and Bousman was basically untried. But, as he did with *Repo*, he used smoke and mirrors to get people's attention. "I had no agents or managers at the time. So, I made up a fake agency, as well as a fake management company. I made fake letterhead, even had a fake voicemail box."

Bousman had a feature horror script he was sending out called *The Desperate*. The screenplay found its way into the hands of film producer Gregg Hoffman, who called Bousman and set up a meeting. "Keep in mind, *Saw* had not come out yet," Bousman said. "Overnight, Gregg's partners, Oren Koules and Mark Burg, read the script. Oren calls Gregg up and says, 'Wait, let's turn *The Desperate* into *Saw II*.'

"Next thing I know, I am meeting at Lionsgate Films (LGF) in a room full of executives. Here's where it gets sticky. *Saw* is tracking huge. Everyone realizes they have a hit on their hands. A sequel is a no-brainer. But who in their right mind would ever hire me... a dude who has directed a bunch of really terrible short films and has been fired from almost every production job he has ever had? I knew the odds of me ever convincing LGF to let me direct this were slim to none. Thank God for Peter Block, an executive at LGF, who bought into what I was selling [because] two months after my meeting, I am on a plane to Toronto to film *Saw II*. Just weeks prior, I was penniless, sleeping on couches and working as a tape room operator dubbing video tapes. Now, I was on a plane to direct a real Hollywood movie."

Saw II opened at No. 1 on October 28, 2005, and was another multi-million-dollar smash. Bousman signed on to do *Saw III* and once again struck gold for LGF when that picture was released a year later. But he really wanted to turn *Repo* into a feature film—his *next* feature film. Naturally, the studio wanted him to make *Saw IV* first. They both got their way, but it didn't turn out quite as either party had hoped.

CHAPTER 3

PRE-PRODUCTION

Following the phenomenal success of *Saw II* and *III*, everyone considered Bousman a shoo-in to direct *Saw IV*—everyone, that is, except for Bousman. He wanted nothing more than to direct his dream project: *Repo.* He'd been talking about the project for years and promising Smith and Zdunich that come hell or high water, he would see it get made. It took both, plus a lot of persuasion and a little game-playing, to get LGF to agree. "I told them I'll direct *Saw IV* if I can make *Repo* at the same time," Bousman said. It was a classic case of "one for you, one for me."

One of the most potent factors in getting LGF to see things his way was a proof-of-concept short film Bousman took it upon himself to make. As a director and friend who engendered great respect and loyalty from those around him, he was able to muster up an impressive presentation with very few resources.

Dan "Spooky" Walker, a film journalist who would later become *Repo*'s documentarian and the road manager for their tours, already knew Bousman when the director was wrapping up *Saw III*. "[Bousman] got his whole crew to stay on after shooting *Saw III*, and they made this short," said Walker. "My first introduction to *Repo* was seeing the short film version. Zdunich reprised his role as Grave Robber, Michael Rooker was the Repo Man, and Shawnee Smith played a combination of Shilo and Amber Sweet. J. LaRose was in it, too."

LaRose met Bousman in the 1990s when both were in film school. He acted in some of Bousman's student and early low-budget productions. "He never forgot me. He cast me in *Saw III* and *IV*—some major films. I'll always appreciate that," said LaRose. He was more than happy to help his friend get the attention of LGF so that *Repo* could get made. "Darren's a charming guy, so he's got all these friends that are willing to try to pitch in and make his madness come to life. David Hackl, the brilliant production designer for the *Saw* films, came in and worked on the short, bringing the world to life. He built stuff out of nothing; it's amazing. So, in the short we sang pieces of the songs, we had a chase scene... it's kind of wacky. The makeup is a little different from what wound up in the feature."

Once the short was done, Bousman still needed to get LGF committed to making *Repo*. "He rented out this fancy-ass Beverly Hills theater to get distributors to show up," Walker recalled. "And he had a handful of us entertainment journalists show up." Walker was working for *BloodyDisgusting.com* at the time. Bousman also conjured up his showman side and made quite an impression. "He had, like, a chick on a gurney, and there were crazy, sexy nurses. *TMZ* showed up, so it was this weird, bizarro night. But it got the rival distributors excited, and that's how LGF finally let him make *Repo*."

Twisted Pictures producers Daniel Heffner, Carl Mazzocone, Mark Burg, and Oren Koules came on board, and Bousman, Smith, and Zdunich got to work in earnest on the script, music, behind-the-camera hires, and casting.

Once that was set, Bousman began thinking about how the *Repo* world should look. "There's so much *Dick Tracy* in *Repo*—including the stage show, where you have these bigger-than-life characters, these very flamboyant, over-the-top sets and lighting designs. I remember when we wrapped the first stage show, I said to Terrance and Darren, 'if I ever have the chance to make this into a movie, I will because it's one of those places I want to live in.'"

At the time, Bousman was dating Laura Bosserman, who would later become his wife. She was also an instrumental creative player during the making of *Repo*—and of course, she offered personal and emotional support. The couple met at a Super Bowl party in February 2006. "*Saw II* had just come out," Laura recalled, "but I didn't go see it because I wasn't into horror films. Darren and I dated for three weeks before he moved to Toronto to do *Saw III*. We had a long-distance relationship for almost nine months. It was extremely difficult, but I knew it would be worth it. I remember in July of 2006, Darren and I met up in San Diego because he was in town for Comic-Con. He was talking to Terrance, whom I had met once in NYC, on the phone. We were in a clothing store, and Darren told Terrance that he was going to follow through with his promise to make *Repo* into a film. I had never seen the stage production, but of course, I had heard all the music from the show. Darren was making a deal with Lionsgate that if he directed *Saw IV*, they would make *Repo.* I started crying in the store because I realized my boyfriend would be going back to Toronto the following year and making two films back-to-back. I had a job at the time, but nothing I would call a career, so I ended up moving to Toronto with Darren for about a year in February 2007."

One of Bousman's many key hires was cinematographer Joseph White. Since the visuals are a huge part of the story, the director needed to work with someone as excited about the project as he was. After lots of discussions, the pair worked on lookbooks and storyboarding. "We drew a lot of inspiration from pretty eclectic films, but we were very much consciously trying to do our own thing," White recalled. "So, you can talk about *Phantom of the Paradise*, you can talk about *Dick Tracy*, you can talk about all that stuff, but we really wanted it to be our own thing. We took inspiration from a lot of those other films—less in terms of how we were building our palette and look and more in terms of, *those* people fucking went for it, we're going to fucking go for it too, but in our own way."

Working on *Repo* together set the pair on a long and fruitful collaboration. White and Bousman had already known each other for years, but it was their first feature as a team. "I was only about twenty-seven at the time," White said, "so it was a huge opportunity for me and a significant jump up in terms of budget. Darren wanted [a DP] who was younger and more willing to sort of go out there and creatively do crazy shit. And I was excited to be a part of it. I got to do something that wasn't a deep shadow, low-budget horror film. It was colorful and eye-catching, and pretty different visually."

David Hackl, production designer on the film and Bousman's *Saw* sequels, was also brought on board. "The first thing Darren said was, 'I don't want this to look like a *Saw* movie.' Certainly, the colors are far brighter than the other *Saw* films, and he wanted it to be a look of its own. We wanted to try and create an entire universe, and I think that we wanted *Repo* to be this otherworldly place; not necessarily Earth in fifty years, but another world altogether."

Zdunich created the comic book panels that set up the story at the beginning of the film, as well as those sprinkled throughout. "There's an animated prologue that I've done to set up the movie," he said. "It explores the question of what does it look like when people start to change themselves in the future? What's the next step beyond plastic surgery?"

Smith added, "Basically, we're touching on the fact that as we're living today in this world, our nervous systems are almost breaking down by the virtual influx of information. Our attentions are split between twenty different things at any given time. And this is what's causing people's bodies in the future to break down and to suffer these plagues. People are dying of this overstimulation, this syndrome that they have. And this is what opens the door for GeneCo. It motivates their rise to power."

"Some of the imagery is pretty extreme," Zdunich explained. "Like, runway models standing in front of X-ray machines, and they have enlarged hearts or bigger kidneys sticking out. And that's vogue. That's chic. It's sick, but it's not just sick for sick's sake. It's based in reality. You can say, 'Yeah, I can see organ repossessions becoming legal somewhere down the road.'"

CASTING

The film's cast is perhaps one of the most eclectic ever assembled, but one thing they all had in common was a background in music. *Repo* stars: Sarah Brightman, the most successful soprano in the world, whose credits include *Phantom of the Opera*, in her first-ever movie role; performance artist Nivek Ogre, best known as the front man for the experimental industrial band Skinny Puppy; Anthony Head, who fans loved from his turn in *Buffy the Vampire Slayer* (including the unforgettable musical episode); Paul Sorvino, a classically trained opera singer in his first movie musical role; Alexa PenaVega, who made her Broadway debut as Penny Pingleton in *Hairspray*;

Paris Hilton, whose debut album *Paris* was released a year before filming and reached #6 on the *Billboard* album chart; and Bill Moseley, who in addition to his well-known horror roles, was also a member of the band Cornbugs with Guns N' Roses guitar player Buckethead.

Alexa PenaVega as Shilo Wallace

PenaVega, then nineteen, first heard about the role via direct messaging by Bousman through the social networking platform MySpace. "This creepy director would not leave me alone, and he kept writing me all these messages that kept saying, 'I want to put you in this movie.' I'm like, who is this weirdo? So finally, I called my agent, and I asked about him because he said he'd directed *Saw*." But James Wan directed *Saw*, and until PenaVega and her reps realized the mix-up, they didn't get back to him. But Bousman was persistent. PenaVega had found great success in the *Spy Kids* film franchise, and in addition to acting, she could sing. Luckily, it all worked out, and Bousman got the *Repo* script to PenaVega. "Then he showed me the little short that they made. As soon as I watched that, I emailed Darren, and I said, 'I have to do this movie.'"

It was Laura who thought of PenaVega for the role. "*Repo* was not only destined for cult status, but it was also *designed* for cult status," Laura explained. "The casting of every single character was incredibly deliberate and serendipitous at the same time. Shilo—Alexa—was first. Darren and I were in our hotel room watching rock opera DVDs like *The Apple* and *Phantom of the Paradise,* and we were scouring the internet for young actresses that could sing. I was reading *The New York Times* and came across an ad for *Hairspray* on Broadway starring *Spy Kids'* Alexa PenaVega as Penny. I said to Darren, 'She's the one!' We flew to NYC the next weekend, watched her steal the show, and fell in love with her upon meeting her."

Although she did appear onstage in 2007 as Penny in *Hairspray*, PenaVega found that singing for celluloid is much different. "Once you record your songs in the studio, you can't change the way it sounds when you're there on set. So, if you have an idea like, oh, I want to try it this way, you can't. You know that whatever you do is set in stone," she said. "What's done is done. So, you have to act accordingly. You can't make a face here and not match with the way you're mouthing it or the way it's been sung. It's definitely a new process for me, but so good."

Anthony Head as Nathan Wallace

While Nathan is not the heart of the movie, his role is perhaps the most demanding because he must be a caring, doting dad in some scenes, then a ruthless organ Repo Man in others, and believable in both.

"Darren wanted Anthony Head from day one," Laura recalled. "The studio made Darren meet bigger stars for the role, and he did meet with Kevin Bacon when we were in NYC seeing *Hairspray*. I remember during the middle of shooting

Saw IV, someone said that Mick Jagger was interested. Darren's assistant flew to NYC and back on the same day to deliver him the DVD of the promotional music video. Mr. Jagger said he didn't like the wigs in the video and therefore shot it down. But it was always going to be Tony Head, and it had to be Tony Head."

Other names were thrown around, including Kevin Costner and Patrick Swayze. Swayze all but accepted the role, then "ghosted" everyone from *Repo*. Jonathan McHugh, one of *Repo*'s executive producers and the music supervisor, tells the story:

"Paris Hilton auditioned, and she killed it. But look, here's the one thing: we had just hired Patrick Swayze as the leading man. And I say to the guys, if you're doing a musical, with Patrick Swayze and Paris Hilton... I know this is a campy film, but you're taking it deeply over the top, right? So, we've got to ask Patrick Swayze what he thinks about Paris Hilton. The next day Patrick comes into the studio, I pull him aside, and I say, 'I just want to ask you, before we pull the trigger, because you're the star, how you feel about this.' He says, 'Hey man, I think everybody needs a second chance, and if you guys feel she is right for the role, I can work with anybody.' I say, 'Are you sure about this?' He says, 'Absolutely.' And I say, 'Okay, but you've got to be sure.' He says, 'I'm sure.' I say, 'Anybody you want to ask? The wife, the publicist?' 'No,' he goes, 'I'm good.' So, I make the call, whatever it is, an hour later, and there's a press release out from Paris Hilton that she's captured this role and she's going to star in *Repo.*

"We were about to shoot in maybe two weeks, so we're auditioning in the studio the next day, and Patrick doesn't show up. So, I call him and call him, and hours later, I get him and say, 'Patrick, you sick?' He's like, 'No.' And I go, 'So let me get this straight, you talked to your wife and your publicist, and they say you shouldn't do the movie, right?' He's silent for a long beat. Then he says, 'I can't do it, man, I'm sorry.'

"I'm so mad. I'm thinking, you're putting the whole production in jeopardy because you have not asked the questions I asked you to ask in advance. So, after we hung up, I wrote this nasty email and blah, blah, blah, and I send it off. Never heard back from him again. Anyway, three months later, it comes out that he's diagnosed with cancer. I always regretted sending that email because maybe in the interim, he got that diagnosis, right? I never forgave myself for that."

Other actors auditioned, but Bousman settled on Anthony Head because of his role in the *Buffy the Vampire Slayer* television series. He felt that fans of *Buffy* would also be fans of *Repo.* "*Buffy*'s like a big, over-the-top kind of gothic show," Bousman said. "'Once More with Feeling,' which was the *Buffy* musical episode, was something I referenced a lot as being a huge inspiration for me."

One of Head's favorite scenes to shoot in *Repo* was the "Thankless Job" song, dance, and death number. "I string someone up and disembowel them while singing," Head said during a press conference to promote the film's release. "And when I say singing, it's like this bizarre showstopper number that reminds me of Tom Waits. It's a great song, but it's one of those that you think, why is this guy enjoying it so much? There is this manic thing in the way he kind of just blanks out on what he's doing, and I hope there's a moment in the film where you see this noble, other side to it. When you read a script, either you identify with the character or, as my teacher in L.A. used to say, you get an organ-reject—one of these parts that you try to identify with, but you can't. This role, for some strange reason, I can identify with quite easily. It's the most extraordinary project I've ever been involved with, and it started with being brought in by someone's love of it. Their commitment is what brought me into it, nothing else. And it's gradually grown into this extraordinary creature."

Sarah Brightman as Blind Mag

Brightman, though a veteran of the worldwide stage, had never acted in a film before coming into the *Repo* world. But, as Brightman said during a press conference, both avenues are similar. "It's really about telling the truth. It's what you are told in the script. What subtext you're given by your director, and how you feel about being in your character and finding the truth. From what I've seen, the camera really picks up whether you're telling the truth or not, so you have to stick to that. There wasn't any transition for me. It was just playing the part."

Terrance Zdunich as Grave Robber

There was never any question about who would play Grave Robber. The actor who wrote and created the role was the obvious choice. "It's a character that originated in one of the ten-minute operas, which essentially was a short story about a futuristic grave robber that was taking not rings and gold fillings but literally stealing DNA from the bodies. In that little short story, he talked about things that he would see in the graveyard, and one of them was this organ Repo Man and his daughter, which is what our story is about."

Paris Hilton as Amber Sweet

Casting celebutant Hilton, who at the time was in jail for violating her probation from a previous DUI offense, was risky. Despite having a recent hit album, she certainly lacked "street cred"—particularly among horror film fans, who'd blasted her performance in the 2006 *House of Wax* remake. Over the years, many movie lovers said they'd refused to even think of seeing *Repo* because of her involvement (and, in many cases, subsequently praised the film and her performance after breaking down and seeing it years later).

It all came down to the fact that Hilton was right for the part. Amber Sweet is an heiress. She's spoiled, looks-obsessed, and has a vulnerable side. Smith said that the studio sent dozens of candidates to audition. "We were blessed with having all these great characters and great actors playing them, but when it came to Amber, casting the so-called Scalpel Slut, we're like, 'all she needs to be is really good-looking and vacuous. That's it.' But the studio hadn't given us a single actress who was even close. It was frustrating. It was like, I can go out to Starbucks on Magnolia, and I can find you five girls there who are really fucking hot! How hard in L.A. is it to get that? So, when Paris Hilton came in, we were like, 'we really don't want to do this, but we'll give her a shot.' And then she just nails the part in the audition."

Years later, despite the backlash, Bousman does not regret casting Hilton. "I met with fifty women for that role. Remember, I was coming off *Saw III*, a very popular film. And I had so many actors that wanted to be in this film. Paris called me from jail, begging to have the chance to audition. Paris was the best. She was the only one that came in to audition dressed as the character. She even had a lookbook of what she felt the world was. She was the most articulate in the room on being able to talk about what it was, and I'm talking about actors twice her caliber. They just felt flighty and were unprepared and didn't know what this was or what they were committing to. She wasn't. She was the opposite of that. And I think that's just her as a businessperson. Business is so serious to her. She came in more prepared, and she won the role for that. She's a fascinating story because I think people think of her as the dumb blonde because that's the role she plays. But that's not who she is at all."

Just before the movie came out, Hilton told the same story to the press. "I met with Darren, and I told him that I really wanted this part. I knew it was going to be a hard part to get because it was something so unlike me and like nothing I had ever been asked to do, so I just really put all my heart and soul into it and really rehearsed every single day and practiced with a voice coach and learned the whole movie and that's why I got the part. I *am* this part and am having such an incredible time. Everyone is so nice.

"Amber is sweet, and she's a very tortured girl. I think the main thing is, she wants attention from her father, who runs GeneCo, this huge corporation. They're very wealthy. You can have all the money in the world, but you can still be unhappy. She gets addicted to Zydrate, this futuristic drug, as well as plastic surgery because she keeps wanting to change her appearance to get attention from her father. It was such an honor to be offered a role like this because I usually get cast as the blonde airhead/blonde bombshell, and I think this time, I was cast as something completely different. It was a lot of fun playing someone who looks nothing like me and playing someone who's so crazy. And the music is fantastic! It was such a fun film to do, and we all became so close in our *Repo* family."

Paul Sorvino as Rotti Largo

Sorvino, who'd acted in serious dramas like *That Championship Season* and *Goodfellas*, jumped at the chance to play the powerful and cruel patriarch of the Largo family. "Something that most people don't know about me is that I'm an operatic tenor. And this is the first time that I get a chance in movies to use my operatic voice, which I have used at the Seattle Opera, the New York City Opera, the Gala at the Met, and concerts. It's a great role as well." Sorvino praised Bousman and the cast and crew, adding, "Never have I seen so many work for so little for so long."

McHugh recalled, "We hired mostly singers. Another one of the producers, Carl Mazzocone, closed Paul Sorvino. We took him out for dinner. We went to this Italian restaurant that he wanted to go to, on Melrose. He tells us that he's a trained opera singer. And as a matter of fact, he may be one of the best opera singers of all time. Like, there's Enrico Caruso, and then there's him, type of shit. Then he literally breaks out into song, singing full opera in the restaurant. It was one of the crazier things I've ever seen."

Nivek Ogre (Kevin Ogilvie) as Pavi Largo

Repo was Ogre's first major role in a film, though he'd always been interested in acting. "My first audition was for the role of Funboy in *The Crow* with Alex Proyas, but I was out of my element in a lot of ways. I had another audition with Alexandre Aja for *The Hills Have Eyes,* and that went really well, so even though I didn't get that role, it kind of bolstered my confidence to try for *Repo*. It was a good day for me."

Ogre found acting relatively straightforward in terms of the over-the-top masked character he had to play. "Skinny Puppy is a theatrical project anyway, so it was an easy fit for me. I've [worn masks], and within Skinny Puppy, we've always used that kind of facade to create characters. So, Pavi became very reflective of my own insecurities."

Laura noted that Ogre was, indeed, very humble and said 'I'm sorry' a lot, even though there was nothing to apologize for. "He is truly the kindest human being and brought a rock-star presence and Canadian kindness."

Bill Moseley as Luigi Largo

When he auditioned, Moseley was already a horror film icon and sang in the band Cornbugs, so it was probably a foregone conclusion that he'd be cast. But which role? He, of course, wanted to play Nathan. "I thought somehow, some way," he said years later. "Anyway, it came down obviously to Anthony, who did a fantastic job. I ended up as Luigi, and it was so much fun.

"During the rehearsals, I got to meet Ogre and just had a great time with him. That was my bromance. What a great guy. And also, I met Paris Hilton early in the process. I remember bringing Marion, my younger daughter, who was about ten at the time, to one of the rehearsals, and Paris put Marion in charge of her dogs. She loved that! Paris was really friendly and nice to Marion, and I certainly appreciated that."

Darren Gordon Smith as Bandleader

Smith has a small role in the film as well. "I found that this acting shit is for the birds when I played the Bandleader. I only had two days of shooting the scene, and I'm running around, jumping, and somebody said, 'Kicking more than necessary.' I was so tired. I was so happy to get back here and sit behind my little producer's desk and do the budget and the music."

Alisa Burket as Henchgirl #2 and J. LaRose as GeneCo Spokesperson

Burket reprised her role from the New York stage play as Rotti Largo's Henchgirl. "It was fun, but damn, my feet were so sore. During filming, it was torture because everything was on a concrete stage, and my counterpart, Andreja Punkris, is 5'10" and I'm 5'7" so I had to wear these platform stiletto boots to be as close to the same height as her. I would be dying in those bitches but holy shit!, we had the most hilarious times together. It was definitely all worth it. And working with Paul Sorvino was a blast."

LaRose was happy to work with his friend Bousman again in his small role as a spokesman for GeneCo. "It was a very cool set, and it usually is on one of Darren's projects because as intense as he can be, he's a fun guy. He's fun to be around. In general, film sets are very stressful, but for me, getting to meet the likes of Sarah Brightman and Nivek Ogre... I already knew Bill, but getting to see Paul Sorvino do his thing and hang out with him a bit, work with him, was great. So that was just a blast for me. And then among all that is this great music going on all the time because there's always music blaring and people dancing or singing. It's just a wonderful, wonderful playground. It definitely had that passion project vibe."

CHAPTER 4

PRODUCTION

There is a term in filmmaking: Hot Set. It indicates a set used for filming that will be used again soon, so it is a warning not to move anything; otherwise, the film's continuity will be compromised. But one day, while filming *Repo*, the term became quite literal.

It was during a highly emotional scene involving PenaVega, Head, and Brightman. "We were about to shoot this scene where I come running down the stairs and dad is fighting with Blind Mag," PenaVega recalled. "I get in the middle of it, and it's this great shot where the camera is panning to each of us, and we are in a triangle yelling at each other. Obviously, we're singing, and they have all the smoke machines blowing outside and the wind going. It's really picking up, and we start getting tense. All of a sudden, we smell this burning, and someone starts yelling, 'Fire! Fire!' and there is a big blaze outside the front door. The set is on fire, and you start to think to yourself, what do I do? That is our exit! You kind of go through this panic. Like a dummy, I run up the stairs and think, great.

I'm trapped. And then the smart Anthony and Miss Sarah Brightman run out the fire escape. There is literally this little fire escape on set, and I'm upstairs with my knitting needles."

Laura was there to capture it all. "When I moved to Toronto with Darren, I had no friends there. It was freezing cold outside, and I was living in the hotel. I was pretty depressed, so I started going to set every single day. *Saw IV* was filmed mainly on a soundstage with production offices upstairs, so I would go from set to Darren's trailer to the production offices—always with Chance the Dog." The couple's beloved flurry white pooch can be seen in many photos and behind-the-scenes footage from the period. "The production offices were going to remain the same for *Repo,* so I made myself at home in an empty office. It was during this time that I began my hands-on experience with film. Darren had started teaching me—just by showing me a million movies—and talking me through them. Darren and I had come up with the idea of my filming the behind-the-scenes of *Repo*, so I used my office as a classroom. I would watch documentaries and other behind-the-scenes featurettes. I bought a book on filmmaking and studied it every day. Darren bought me a camera, and I pored over the instruction manual. But, the best learning experience of all was watching Darren in action, working."

By all accounts, there was never a dull moment during filming. "It was like a party at all times," Bousman said. "It was kind of like a circus; you would walk on our set and see a million things. We had tents, carnival performers, popcorn machines, little people, men on stilts, and fire eaters. And this was just one part of the set. Go ten feet over, and we had a massive Victorian graveyard. On top of that, there was blaring music at all times and half-naked women everywhere. It was awesome."

When the women weren't half-naked, some misbehaved in the most playful, benign ways. Moseley recalls Hilton deviating from the script to grab his crotch during the "Mark It Up" dance sequence, just to make him laugh because he'd realized he was not in sync during the number. "Our choreographer, Tré Armstrong, was trying to get everybody to follow her steps. I immediately realized that if I'm by myself, I'm fine, but trying to do choreography with others, I've got two left feet. So, I added that to Luigi's character traits. But Paris, Ogre, and I all had chemistry. Even though Paris was pretty much the big star of the cast, she was willing to play."

Hilton's celebrity was a lot to contend with. Even though the shoot took place in Toronto, Canada, fans and paparazzi were everywhere. It was even more of a sideshow prior to principal photography when, in Los Angeles, the cast prerecorded their songs. The happily married Smith recalled helping Hilton carry some things from the music studio to her car and getting a kiss on the cheek in thanks. Within minutes, the photos were all over the internet speculating about "Paris' new man."

Speaking of new men, Ogre's character, Pavi, loves to reinvent himself by donning a new face every other day using the repo'd faces of various women indebted to GeneCo. The main mug he wears throughout the film comes from a cast of Laura's face. The ghostly white second skin was stretched taut by bolts affixed to Pavi's cheeks, forehead, and chin, leaving only his dark eyes visible.

"When the FX guys made the mask for him, they cast my face... this is me," Bosserman told the press during the set visit.

Ogre added, "She loves herself."

Laura laughed, then kissed his (her?) cheek. "I don't remember whose idea it was to use my face as one of his in the film, but Darren was always throwing me into something. I once had to do a voice-over for a girl being raped in *Saw IV*, and Darren's parents were standing just ten feet away." Talk about awkward. "I'm glad they used my face because it was nice meeting *Repo* fans on tour who were dressed as Pavi," she added.

This is where I come in. As I mentioned in the *Introduction*, my own entry to the wild, warped world of *Repo* was during a set visit at the tail end of filming.

Press Corps Set Visit

I flew in from Los Angeles to Toronto on Friday, October 12, 2007, to observe—along with my fellow members of the press—the very last bit of filming on *Repo*, plus do a *Saw IV* press junket and preview screening. We were given a tightly structured schedule, as follows:

6:00 PM *REPO* SET VISIT

Darren Smith, screenwriter and cocreator of original musical production, will serve as a tour guide. No formal interviews will be conducted on set, but the cast will meet and greet as production allows. No press video or still cameras allowed. LGF will provide B-roll for broadcast outlets when the embargo is lifted on October 29, along with stand-up footage shot with our crew on-site. Embargo agreements will be provided to sign on-site.

8:00 PM *SAW IV* SCREENING

The first seventy-five minutes of *Saw IV* (minus the twist ending) will be shown. Note that the footage is being screened from DV Cam format and is not a final-mixed, color-corrected version of the film. For these reasons, reviews are prohibited—screening is for interview preparation purposes only.

Saturday, October 13

7:30 AM LGF hospitality suite opens, breakfast is served

8:00 AM — *REPO*! TV INTERVIEWS
9:15 AM Participants: Paris Hilton & Darren Bousman (paired)

9:15 AM — *REPO*! PRESS CONFERENCE
10:00 AM Participants: Darren Bousman, Sarah Brightman, Mark Burg, Anthony Head, Paris Hilton, Oren Koules, Bill Moseley, Nivek Ogre, Paul Sorvino, Alexa PenaVega, Terrance Zdunich

10:00 AM — 10:45 AM	*SAW IV* PRESS CONFERENCE Participants: Mark Burg, Oren Koules, Tobin Bell, Lyriq Bent, Betsy Russell, Scott Patterson
11:00 AM — 1:00 PM	*SAW IV* TV INTERVIEWS Participants: Tobin Bell, Betsy Russell, Lyriq Bent, Scott Patterson

The *Repo* set visit was conducted by Smith and Zdunich, and the two made a great impression right away—it was apparent they'd worked hard to bring their story to life, but there was also a sense of irreverence and fun. Zdunich was still partially in character with his Grave Robber hair extensions. Smith said, "He's a cross between Cyndi Lauper and Betsey Johnson." Zdunich grinned and added, "An *evil* cross!" It was one of the most joyous set visits I'd ever been on, maybe because there wasn't the pressure of a big-budget film. Not to mention the circus-like atmosphere Bousman described; he was not exaggerating.

The first set we saw was the one about to be used—GeneCo's opera house, the site of the scene leading up to the climax of *Repo*. Cast, crew, and 400 extras were preparing. The stage was set with a red carpet, archways, chandeliers, lush velvet curtains, Greek statues, and realistic-looking wrought iron gates. Zdunich said, "What you'll see is a fair leading up to the opera, and in this fair, people are having facelifts and other procedures. Then they'll cut the tape to open the gates to the opera house, and everyone will rush in to watch the show." Smith added, "I just love having Sarah Brightman and Paris Hilton singing together in the same scene!"

We were shown the mostly dismantled graveyard a few feet away (which had previously been used for *Saw IV*), and beyond that was the partial set of the Wallaces' Victorian-style home. We also saw the "Repo Man training room," where saran-wrapped corpses were hung and suspended like punching bags in a gym, ready to be surgically plundered. An ominous vintage dentist's chair was stationed in the middle of the room.

After that, we paid a visit to prop master Jim Murray, who showed us the Zydrate gun he'd fashioned and explained that after going through several color choices, Bousman had settled on the long-lasting blue liquid from glowsticks (green had been considered, but decided against, as it was too similar to *Ghostbusters*). Murray explained, "Zydrate is extracted out of the head at death. They crack the skull and jab [a needle in] the brain cavity and suck this blue liquid out. Then that is the drug you inject into somebody else."

We saw boxes of fake organs (made of silicon, rubber, K-Y Jelly, and blood syrup), bins marked "death pills," bloody rags, and bottles labeled: edible blood, flowing blood, clotty blood. "These are all made out of rubber latex, but for some of the scenes, if we were rushed, we did go and get animal brains, tongues, hearts, and livers because once they're sealed, they're safe." There was also a large photo of a man from the neck down wearing only a teeny pair of Speedos. Murray chuckled when I asked about it and replied, "That's a long story."

Murray told us that the Repo Man does his work in a dark disguise. "He's the Batman of the show, and we had to get the costume right." He opened a leather satchel and showed us an assortment of devices, spikes, and scalpels. "We have leeway here because Repo Man is this crazy character who is a doctor and a surgeon. We built his mask and based it on a paintball mask and then basically added plastic and leather all over it. Then we built-in LED lights so his eyes could be lit up, top and bottom. That way, you can't really see who it is, but there's illumination."

Smith and Zdunich then showed us some concept art. One particularly gruesome piece showed Repo Man tearing out someone's spine. "There are some scenes even more brutal than that, and yes, there's somebody with his entire organs being taken out," Smith told us. "During one scene, 'Thankless Job,' you'll see our Repo Man is tortured because he's got some conflicts, but then he becomes sadistic and does a soft-shoe routine saying, 'It's a thankless job' while he's skinning the muscles inch by inch, tearing off the tissue as he has this poor guy strapped in a wheelchair while he's repossessing all of the organs."

After about an hour of touring and chatting with Smith and Zdunich, we were led back to the opera set. Poster bills lining the carnival row bore various headlines, like "Zydrate Addicts Support Meeting" and "Napoleon's Body Parts." Others encouraged us to "Replace Your Face!" and "Resist Z!" It was hard to see all the details due to the milling, colorful crowd of extras plucked from the local goth scene. Punks, ravers, and drag queens were all clad in latex, metal, velvet, and leather. One woman wore a sky-high Marie Antionette-style wig. A hunched man hobbled around with an oxygen tank in tow. Someone clutched a ragged doll, and another held high a sun umbrella festooned with tassels made of skulls. There was a man with a hat and a Zorro-like mask, another fellow wore sparkly chain mail, and there were even a few members of the press who'd been recruited to help fill the fabricated grand hall. The scene they were lining up for was the ribbon-cutting ceremony heralding the opera house's opening.

We watched and took notes as Bousman laid out the next scene, which would feature Blind Mag and Rotti Largo. The petite, luminous Brightman was resplendent in a metal tiara and wore a green ruched gown accented with leather and studs. Sorvino donned a Meatloaf-like ponytail, a cravat, a regal long jacket, and black boots. His Henchgirls, we were told, are genetically engineered. The pair wore rifles across their backs, crisp white shirts, black jackets, black shorts with fishnets, black boots, and dark wraparound shades offset by slicked hair.

Zdunich said, "The last twenty minutes of the movie take place in this opera house. The main villain of the stories has orchestrated it so that all these characters' lives and conflicts sort of collide at the opera, on stage before a televised audience. So, you have a Roman gladiator-type of show-within-a-show, with a feed-the-Christians-to-the-lions type of thing. You have a blood-thirsty crowd cheering on the death and dismemberment of various people. I think you'll walk away hopefully feeling disgusted by it or just enjoying the gore, but then also walking away really caring for the main character, who climbs out of blood. Or will she?"

Even though there's a lot of red stuff in *Repo*, the film's color palette plays up bright, bold primary colors. "We used a lot of gels," cinematographer Joe White recalled years later. White used special gels created by Vittorio Storaro, a legendary lenser who shot *The Bird with the Crystal Plumage* for Dario Argento and *Apocalypse Now* for Francis Ford Coppola. "The Storaro gels had amazing interpretation and use of color, so we used only his series of gels. They're very thick and very exaggerated and like big colors. There's not a lot of subtlety of color in *Repo*; very much by design. And [we tried] to use color, not just to differentiate sets and environment, but to underscore and underline what was happening in the scene and the moments. There were colors associated with the characters, and we peppered them throughout different scenes and used them as a means of foreshadowing. And to be honest, there was an element of we're just going to do fucking crazy colors."

Repo was the first of many films Bousman and White would do together. "If you took three random films, say *Repo*, *11-11-11*, or *St. Agatha*, none of those films look anything alike. They're all different formats, different locales—whether all exterior or all interior—and different color palettes. What's cool about Darren is that his style is more about his process and less about a 'look,' per se. He loves transitions, and he likes a lot of camera movement, stuff like that. But visually, the through line is a little harder to nail down because he likes to challenge himself. I think that ties into him as a friend because he needs to be able to feel comfortable trying all this stuff out. Working in all these different environments with friends, I think, is incredibly, incredibly important to him. That's because your collaborators have your back when the days get long and the call sheets get longer. We've done projects that were successful and less successful, but he's just a fucking incredibly decent, funny, best friend you could hope to have in your life."

While the look of *Repo* may seem wild and unfettered, that freedom was quite contained. Everything was built on the soundstage by Hackl and his team, then expanded upon by the digital team in post, plus storyboarded to the nth degree. Since the actors prerecorded all their songs in the studio, they had to be able to lip-sync their lines flawlessly to accommodate for close-ups and stay within the predetermined mood.

Aftermath

While *Repo* was being made, there was a bit of a dustup regarding a suspiciously similar sci-fi movie called *Repo Men. Repo Men* was based on a 2009 novel called *Repossession Mambo*, so it was simple math to conclude that *Repo*—with its stage version debuting in 2001—was first. But doubts persisted.

Smith recalled, "Universal Studios picked up *Repo Men*, and they tried to get ahead of us by putting out a thing in *Variety*. I think we just beat them. But when the *Variety* thing came out saying Jude Law and Forest Whitaker are gonna star in this upcoming film, blah, blah, blah, we got calls from the producers from LGF and Twisted Pictures. They're like, 'you guys didn't steal this, did you?'

"We were both filming at the same time in Toronto. Across the way, across the railroad tracks, was another huge soundstage. They were filming *Repo Men* over there, and the word on the set was that they were trying to poach our crew." No one moved over to the higher-paying big studio production, though—as ever, Bousman engendered loyalty in his crew.

Smith says there was no question of changing *Repo*'s name to *The Necromerchant's Debt* or something similar. "We never really had a title that we were one thousand percent on while doing our stage shows from 2001 to 2005. By the time of our short in 2006, we were resolute on the present name, and we weren't going to change it because of them. In any event, there was already a *Repo Man* movie from the '80s, so we were okay with that."

While *Repo Men* is not a musical, the similarities were striking. In addition to sharing the same basic concept of Repo Men taking back human organs bought on credit, both films feature an addictive painkiller that glows. In *Repo*, it's the blue liquid of "Z" or "Zydrate," whereas, in *Repo Men,* it's "Q," made from a red powder.

Repo Men was released about two years after *Repo*, but the fervent 40,000-strong "Repo Army" that had formed encouraged a boycott of the Universal film. Bousman wrote in his blog, "I consider myself lucky to have such a rabid fan base as the Repo Army. I hope and urge them all to support *Repo Men*, as it helps bring awareness to our movie as well. In the end, we are all artists here, in love with our art. Bashing *Repo Men* is the exact opposite thing that I want fans to do... *Repo* is about acceptance, not alienation."

CHAPTER 5

MUSIC

With more than ninety minutes of music and forty-eight original tunes, *Repo* was widely reported to have the most music of any American production in film history. That's quite a feat, especially considering the timeline—a mere two months to complete everything so it would be ready for principal photography.

Repo's soundtrack and score recording took place at Extasy Recording Studio in Los Angeles' San Fernando Valley in North Hollywood. Chris Spilfogel, whose credits include *Dreamgirls* and *Hairspray*, was the Chief Recording Engineer and the music's assistant producer. Yoshiki Hayashi from the legendary rock band X Japan produced the music with composer Joseph Bishara, who is now best known for his iconic scores for James Wan's *The Conjuring* and *Insidious* franchise films.

"I did not see the stage play," Bishara recalled. "The first time I heard about *Repo* was seeing Darren Bousman posting a bit online; then, a mutual friend brought me in. They were already set up at Yoshiki's studio at that point and had a lot to do in a short amount of time. I met the whole team one night, and we started the next day. It was just kind of like, 'All right, go!'

"That was before the film was shot, and the deadline was looming. The vocals *were* the performances, so those had to be not only recorded, but edited and assembled. Darren essentially had to direct the performance from the voices before he got to set. That was a challenge."

At this point, Smith and Zdunich were heavily, intensively involved. "Those two have an interesting dynamic working together," Bishara observed. "They complemented each other really well. Darren's style is anything goes—he's almost doing cartwheels through a stack of instruments, and he just kind of bursts into the room and makes this crazy music. Terrance is much more calculated. He very much thinks things through. Before doing anything, he's definitely put a lot of thought and energy into it. So, you put those two together, and it creates an interesting energy."

There were a lot of personalities involved, but the process was harmonious. Among the musicians featured were Richard Patrick (Filter), Stephen Perkins (Jane's Addiction), Shawn "Clown" Crahan (Slipknot), Ray Luzier (Korn), Brian Young (David Lee Roth's band), Richard Fortus (Guns N' Roses), Sonny Moore (soon to change his name to Skrillex), David J (Bauhaus, Love and Rockets), Daniel Ash (Love and Rockets), Rob "Blasko" Nicholson (Ozzy Osborne), Tommy Clufetos (Rob Zombie band), Melora Creager (Rasputina), and Rami

Jaffee (Wallflowers). Also lending her voice to the soundtrack was pop star Poe, and Joan Jett played a guitar solo (and appeared in the film) on the high-energy anthem, "Seventeen" (performed by PenaVega). Together they created a diverse, intense collection of songs that blended seamlessly into the horrific rock opera.

In addition to the variety of performers, the opera itself featured Nine Inch Nails-type industrial rock ("21st Century Cure"), Italian and German opera ("Chromaggia" and "Mag's Crucifixus"), punk ("Seventeen"), Tom Waits-inspired cabaret ("Thankless Job"), hip-hop electronica ("Chase the Morning"), Asian pop ("Tao of Mag"), a tender ballad ("I Didn't Know I'd Love You So Much"), jazz ("Buongiorno!"), a comical, techno-Renaissance troubadour tune ("Blame Not My Cheeks"), as well as elements from traditional musicals ("Gold" and "Sawman's Lament"). The music ranges from simple songs to complicated time signatures and harmonies. It utilizes traditional rock instrumentation with ethnic instruments (saz, koto, sitar, oud), 1960s/1970s modular synthesizers, opera choirs, symphonic strings, jazz horn sections, noise generators, fretless guitars, Optigans, and even an assortment of handmade instruments invented by Smith. Each main character also had a motif and usually a specific instrument that played it, like the pianoforte trills used for many of Pavi's entrances during the film.

Burket, who'd been along for the ride since the off-Broadway play days—and would play one of Rotti's Henchgirls in the film—was also involved in the soundtrack's production due to her introduction to Bishara, who would go on to hire her as his assistant. The two worked together for many years.

"I was super grateful to have been a part of the music pre-production team and got to work with the amazingly talented and dedicated engineers and music producers and also the musicians that came through to lay down layers of tracks," Burket said. "To be in the studio from day one of recording, doing everything from coffee and lunch runs to cleaning the studio before artists came in to record, making music spreadsheets and copies, comping vocal and instrumental tracks with the music producers and engineers and then running it all by Darren, Terrance, and Darren Bousman for approval or edits... it was both utterly exhausting and absolutely fulfilling to be a part of that process."

Hilton's songs needed to be edited together from several different takes—like Frankensongs. McHugh recalled putting everything together as brutal. "She's not a real singer. She's an auto-tune singer. And without that, it was a ton of work to get her to sound right. Definitely a challenge. But she brought this incredible sex appeal to the role. And notoriety."

McHugh gathered most of the musical talent and brought Yoshiki on board as a collaborator and investor. One of his coolest additions to the menagerie of performers was Joan Jett. "I asked her to be in the movie when I was working with her band on another thing. I saw that they were going to be in Toronto when we were shooting, so I booked her, and she had a cameo in the film itself. But other people performed the song on the record."

Moseley recalled when he was cast, Darren Bousman quipped that he knew Moseley could kill, but could he sing? "And I said, 'Well, I gave you that Cornbugs CD.' And without missing a beat, he said, 'Yes, but can you sing?' And so being hired was contingent on my passing the singing audition at Yoshiki's studio in North Hollywood." He was given "Night Surgeon" to sing. Apparently, that was the hardest song to master. "They didn't mess around."

Moseley had been taking singing lessons weekly for years (and still does), so he took it to his teacher, and they practiced. "We went over it and talked about it in terms of how to present the song, dramatically build up to it, and just get familiar with it. So, I had that under my belt, and I went to go to the audition. I remember stopping at a little pizzeria beforehand and having a piece of pizza and a can of cola just to get my throat moist and settle my nerves and get something in my stomach. And I went into the studio, and there was Darren, Terrance, Joe Bishara, and Terrance's cowriter—the other Darren. And they were in the control room of the studio, looking down through glass onto the studio floor. And there was a Pussycat Doll there, belting out one of the songs and doing a great job. Sounded throaty and putting her heart into it, she had some moves… she was a pro. And I was thinking, holy shit! I'm screwed."

Of course, they were up for different roles, but Moseley knew she was a hard act to follow. He gave it all he had. "I looked up at the window and saw all these faces in a darkened room looking down at me, and they were smiling and giving me the thumbs up," he said. "So that was basically how I got the job. I think there was a period where they were thinking maybe I would play the main character, Nathan, that Anthony did."

Laura was there to capture everything on camera as the soundtrack was being put together. She recalled what it was like getting to know everyone and shared some of her fun memories. "We had the best time. I was at each rehearsal and recording session with my camera—in the booth, in the studio, in the office. Once we were all in Toronto [for principal photography], I was with the cast and crew all the time, and it felt like we were a family. The cast was staying at a hotel in the middle of downtown, but Darren and I had rented a house in an area called The Beaches. We used to host parties at our house—we'd watch movies, play Guitar Hero, eat, drink, and so on. Alexa was so young, and she became like my little sister. I still call her my Pocket Baby to this day because I felt like I could put her in my pocket and just feed her Skittles, and she would be happy. I remember one night going out clubbing with Paris Hilton—this was at the height of her powers—and we took a black SUV to the club, blasting her song 'The Stars are Blind.' She was impressed that I knew all the words."

In addition to the set visit and several events, including Comic-Con, I was able to cover the launch party for the soundtrack. On a Friday night, the weekend before the official soundtrack for the rock and roll sci-fi horror operatic film was to be released, an outrageous assortment of garish ghouls showed up at the Abbey, a popular West Hollywood watering hole, to help ring in the party.

Hilton entered the jam-packed jamboree wearing a skin-tight black catsuit corset, and she never strayed far from her then-boyfriend, Benji Madden of the band Good Charlotte. She was seemingly everywhere at the time, promoting *Repo*, the comedy film *The Hottie & the Nottie*, and her MTV reality show, *Paris Hilton's My New BFF*. Shortly after her arrival, she stood and addressed the house, along with her director and costars, announcing how proud she was of *Repo* and encouraging everyone to see it on the big screen. While Hilton didn't bust a lung singing anything that night, we did get a few do-re-mi's from Bousman, PenaVega, Ogre, and Moseley.

Despite the generally warm reception for the music, mainstream publications didn't review the soundtrack. But genre and indie websites embraced it. Here are two of the most comprehensive, well-thought-out reviews:

Repo! The Genetic Opera Soundtrack Review / Keith Olexa, *Horror.com*

May Nathan Wallace take anyone's eyes out who hasn't yet seen the heart-pumping, blood-red, *Hellraiser*-meets-*Rent* body bag bonanza provocatively titled, *Repo! The Genetic Opera*. But may he take the ears and eyes of anyone who hasn't even heard it yet.

Why? Because *Repo*'s a movie that's all about the music. It's a manic musical operation that just gets under the skin, only to blow its way out like so many incredible acoustic hemorrhages. It's so good it doesn't need the whole movie to work; the soundtrack puts its hooks in, like metal into skin.

Repo is a brilliantly outlandish patchwork of bruised gothic beats, razor-wire ballads, and postapocalyptic chorales, all stitched together in rigorously operatic tapestry, which in toto is so irreverently distinctive as to almost defy classification. Each track screams aggressively to be "its own thing," yet when united under their grisly theme, comes together as a kind of aural Frankenstein mosaic, a monster of sound and fury that's certainly like no rock opera before it. *Repo* is science fiction at its most obscene and horror at its most lyrical. It's lurid, silly, wild, a little retarded, and it'll kill ya, but in a good way.

Repo's storyline is as simple as a heart attack: in the not-too-distant future, an epidemic of organ failures devastates civilization. One black light in this darkness is GeneCo, a biotech company that specializes in organ transplants. But times are still tough, so when organ transplantees default on their bill payments, GeneCo sends out Repo Men to "reclaim" their merchandise. Amid this surgically sensual setting, a sheltered young girl with a rare disease waxes rebellious and goes out to uncover her family's mysterious past... learning more than she expected to in the process.

Repo the film rose, it seemed, almost organically, like some mutant by-blow of torture porn, soft-core porn, and Soviet-inspired Herschell Gordon Lewis-style horror. That it did this at all is amazing enough by itself, but that it was also allowed to roam the Earth as a musical is either the result of super-science, sorcery, or the brilliance of longtime collaborators and *Repo* screenwriters, Darren Smith and Terrance Zdunich, mixed with a (un)healthy dose of *Saw II*, *III* and *IV* director Darren Lynn Bousman. Whatever the reason, the gorgeous rock opera monstrosity that is *Repo* survived and thrived.

But as a rock opera, *Repo*'s music is the story. The entire film is sung, and each song provides not only plot but also emotional anchors and embellishments to the entire story. Writers Smith and Zdunich seem to understand this very well, as the *Repo* soundtrack practically drips with well-conceived bursts of violence, humor, and pathos.

Soundtrack highlights include "At the Opera Tonight," a tight little piece that's part shrill Fiona Apple and part placid Till Lindemann, with an industrial beat that's about as hard-driving.

"Mark It Up" twists a traditional rock opera sound by cramming the song's lyrics with enough invective and obscenity to make a mafia organ donor blush. Amber Sweet (Paris Hilton), Luigi Largo (Bill Moseley), and Pavi Largo (Skinny Puppy's Nivek Ogre) bust this expositive swear-fest out with measured, talky beats, making this track one of the more offbeat ones, ironically.

"Seventeen" lightens things up, though only in comparison to *Repo*'s other tracks. It's a frenetic rally for little girl emancipation sung by Shilo (Alexa PenaVega) to the sound of heavy electronic chords demanding equal time (it doesn't hurt that Joan Jett is playing on this track as well).

In contrast to that feminist punk-out is the pop-gothic duet "Chase the Morning," sung by Shilo and Blind Mag (Sarah Brightman). The syncopation and lyrics in this song alone make it memorable, to say nothing of Brightman's melodic voice.

Slightly less impressive is "Zydrate Anatomy." It's an intriguing ensemble piece, but Zdunich's Grave Robber doesn't sell the recitative well, and the song misses beats with its affected repeats and multisyllabic science-y lyrics, but it is notable for one thing: Paris Hilton! Her lush, sexy voice matches wits with the slow, somewhat ponderous rhythm of this track and comes out the winner. She puts plenty of welcome heat in what's basically a "how to get an injection" song.

Getting back to notable notes, however, "Night Surgeon" cuts to the quick, clutching at those classic rock opera roots, a la *Hair* and *Jesus Christ Superstar*, with its faintly gospel-sounding chorus and Wallace's sinister Judas gloats. But this track, like the others, threatens to tear the roots out, and Head is partially responsible. He sings like Sweeny Todd on a bender here, but with tremendous heart as well.

But even "Night Surgeon" barely holds a candle to possibly the best track on the entire album, "Legal Assassin." This is a showpiece track for sure and a showstopper for Head. As Giles, this *Buffy the Vampire Slayer* alum hinted in several episodes as to his singing chops, but he really owns those chops here; like a sonorously sanguine Dr. Jekyll, Head turns alternately good and nasty as doting father/body farmer and Wallace's dreadful schism couldn't be more abruptly or starkly revealed than in this agonized paean to a tragically chopped up life.

Such examples litter the *Repo* soundtrack; too many to cite, in fact. *Repo* boasts a staggering number of songs, possibly more than any rock opera ever produced. And while they won't all appeal to every listener, it would be difficult to argue that each isn't shocking, affecting, and unforgettable in its own way. *Repo* may be a sign of the next evolution in listening, and if that's so, I'm joining the evolution.

Repo! The Genetic Opera Soundtrack Review / Dave Manack, *Dread Central*

Over the past few years, movie soundtracks, especially in the horror genre, have become little more than showpieces for a record company's latest "hot" artists. Sadly, the songs and bands on these soundtracks have absolutely nothing to do with the movie itself but are instead filled with flavor-of-the-day acts meant to increase a movie's hip factor with the PG-13 crowd.

But the soundtrack for *Repo! The Genetic Opera* is far more than simply a collection of irrelevant songs from throwaway rock bands. In many ways, the soundtrack for this horrific "rock opera" is the movie, as each song is an integral part of the storytelling process. These tracks are not musical diversions; they feature key dialogue and reveal plot points that the viewer (or, in this case, the listener) would be lost without. This is *Rocky Horror Picture Show* meets *The Wall*—only darker and just a tad more violent.

For those still unfamiliar with this truly one-of-a-kind movie, *Repo* is a futuristic horror musical scheduled for release on November 7, 2008, and has already been described as an instant cult classic. As the plotline states, in the year 2056, an epidemic of organ failures devastates the planet. Out of the tragedy, a savior emerges: GeneCo, a biotech company that offers organ transplants... for a price. Those who miss their payments are scheduled for "repossession" and hunted by villainous Repo Men.

In a world where surgery addicts are hooked on painkilling drugs and murder is sanctioned by law, a sheltered young girl, Shilo (Alexa PenaVega), searches for the cure to her own rare disease as well as information about her family's mysterious history. After being sucked into the haunting world of GeneCo, she is unable to turn back, as all her questions will be answered at the wildly anticipated spectacular event: The Genetic Opera.

In addition to PenaVega, the film features a very talented cast, including Paul Sorvino, Anthony Head, Bill Moseley, Sarah Brightman, and (gasp!) the oft-maligned Hollywood debutante Paris Hilton. It's especially interesting to note that because this is a true "rock opera," each character actually has to sing his/her part—and no one gets off the hook, not even Hilton. But each actor is up to the challenge; Sorvino effectively croons in the track "Gold," PenaVega displays a punk rock edge in "Seventeen," and Head shines in "Legal Assassin," memorably exclaiming, "I am only living out a lie!" Even Hilton manages to impress, as evidenced by her taunts of *Repo*'s Grave Robber character in the song "Can't Get It up if the Girl's Breathing" [eventually cut from the film, but readily available online].

Not surprisingly, however, it is Brightman (who plays Blind Mag) who provides the majority of the standout performances. Brightman, who has starred in such well-known Broadway shows as *Cats* and *Phantom of the Opera*, displays her exceptional operatic talents throughout the soundtrack, and it would not be a stretch to think that her efforts in *Repo* could garner her yet another Grammy nomination. Songs like "Crucifixus," "Chromaggia," and "At the Opera Tonight" showcase exactly why Brightman has become a platinum-selling artist.

Even though *Repo* hasn't even hit theaters yet, it's still a must-have for curious listeners and those eagerly anticipating its release. We have never seen—or in this case, heard—anything quite like *Repo*. In a time when movie soundtracks have become stale and predictable, it's refreshing to see true artists given the opportunity to actually take some chances and produce something that is both unique and memorable.

✖✖✖

It is believed that *Repo* has more sung songs than any other film musical, at least up to 2009. Smith also said that "though it's not in the soundtrack, two songs are played during the credits. The first is a song by Yoshiki, and the other is 'Aching Hour,' a song that I wrote either all or most of and is sung by Sarah Brightman. I recorded her singing that in Hamburg in the winter of 2008."

Soundtrack Listing

1. Comic Book Prologue
2. Genetic Repo Man – Grave Robber
3. Mag's Crucifixus (voicover during flyover city) – Blind Mag, German Chorus
4. Things You See in a Graveyard Part I – Rotti, Mourners
5. 21st Century Cure – Grave Robber, Shilo
6. Shilo Waking from Dream – Shilo, Nathan
7. Infected – Shilo
8. Legal Assassin – Nathan
9. Mark It Up – Luigi, Pavi, Amber Sweet
10. Tao of Mag – Blind Mag
11. Things You See in a Graveyard Part II – Rotti, Mourners
12. Rotti & Shilo Inside Limo – Rotti, Shilo
13. Thankless Job – Nathan/Repo Man
14. Genterns – Genterns, Luigi, Pavi & Blind Mag
15. Luigi, Pavi & Amber Harass Mag – Luigi, Pavi, Amber Sweet, Blind Mag, Rotti
16. Seeing You Two Stirs Memories – Rotti

17. Statue Unveiling – Rotti, Blind Mag, Shilo
18. Nathan & Shilo on Telephone – Nathan/Repo Man, Shilo
19. Zydrate *Repo*rter Interviews Rotti – Zydrate Reporter, Rotti
20. Grave Robber & Shilo Escape from Tent – Shilo, Grave Robber
21. Zydrate Anatomy – Grave Robber, Amber Sweet, Shilo, Zydrate Support Group
22. Who Ordered Pizza? – Luigi, Pavi, Amber Sweet, Nathan, Rotti
23. Night Surgeon – Luigi, Pavi, Rotti, Nathan/Repo Man, Genterns
24. Chase the Morning (remix) – Shilo, Blind Mag
25. Everyone's A Composer – Shilo, Blind Mag, Nathan
26. Come Back! – Shilo, Nathan
27. What Chance Has A 17-Year-Old Girl? – Shilo, Nathan
28. Seventeen – Shilo
29. Happiness Is a Warm Scalpel – Rotti, Amber Sweet
30. Gold – Rotti
31. Nathan Discovers Rotti's Plan – Nathan, Shilo
32. Tonight We Are Betrayed – Nathan/Repo Man
33. At the Opera Tonight – The Ensemble
34. Bloodbath! (Middlelogue) – Grave Robber
35. We Started This Opera Shit – Bandleader, Genterns, Luigi, Pavi, Rotti, Opera Patrons
36. Rotti's Interrogation Room Challenge – Rotti
37. Buongiorno! – Rotti, Luigi, Pavi, Genterns
38. Blame Not My Cheeks – Amber Sweet

39. Chromaggia – Blind Mag
40. Rotti's Pièce de Résistance – Rotti
41. Let the Monster Rise – Nathan/Repo Man, Shilo
42. Sawman's Lament – Shilo, Nathan, Rotti, Luigi, Pavi, Opera Patrons
43. May I Introduce Made You Sick – Shilo, Rotti, Nathan
44. Cut The Ties Completely – Shilo, Rotti, Nathan, Luigi, Pavi
45. Shilo Turns Against Rotti – Shilo, Nathan, Rotti
46. I Didn't Know I'd Love You So Much – Shilo, Nathan
47. Genetic Emancipation – Shilo
48. Epilogue – Grave Robber

CHAPTER 6
RECEPTION

Test Screening

"One of the worst parts of being a filmmaker is when you have to have a film tested," Bousman said. "Testing is when the studios take an unreleased film to a smaller city, usually outside of L.A., and ask a variety of people from different walks of life, different ethnicities, and different age ranges to watch and rate your film. When we had the first test screening of *Repo*, we were abysmal in the testing. I don't remember what the exact number was, but I want to say it was around 8% and what you want is around 70%-80% of the people to embrace the film and believe in it and to say they would recommend it to a friend. In our case, less than 10% of the people liked the movie."

Smith recalled, "That screening was in Chatsworth. In the San Fernando Valley. It was an eye-opener, quite honestly. We were all in this *Repo* bubble, where everybody involved in the process thinks, 'this is the best thing ever!' But after that market screening, LGF didn't even want to release the film in theaters. They said it should go straight to DVD."

McHugh remarked, "I never understood why they didn't research it at the Sunset 5, the Laemmle, or some alternative theaters and bring those people out. This movie needed nurturing; it needed a buildup. And obviously [Lionsgate] didn't believe in it, so they didn't really put any marketing money into it. Or muscle. If we could have just gotten the film company to get behind it, even in the afterlife, it would have been so much bigger. And that's what's frustrating for me about it. You see it all. You're a part of it. You know what it *could* be."

Bousman added, "There was this collective kind of letdown. You felt the air deflate, and all of the hope kind of left the room at the end of that screening. I saw very rapidly that I was not going to have a lot of support at LGF. And I get it now, but at the time that it happened, I was very vocal and angry. But it's a business, right? It's a business decision. Here's a company that had to put millions behind a movie to get it out to the public. So why would they want to put thirty million dollars behind a movie when basically, less than 10% of the audience would go to see it?"

But, Bousman clarified, *Repo* was at a distinct disadvantage going into such a screening—the movie wasn't ready. "All we had was the editor's assemblage, which meant the final music wasn't in there. There were no visual effects yet, and it was kind of... haphazardly put together because LGF wanted to know what they had. So, it could not have gone worse. But I knew that the music was going to change everything, and when the visual effects were put in, there would be an audience for it."

Bousman said he strongly felt that *Repo* would find its niche in the same subgenres that included his favorite films. "Like *Tommy*. If you go back and watch *Tommy* again, you will see that it is batshit crazy. From Elton John and his twenty-thousand-size shoes and his ridiculous glasses to Ann-Margret being covered in baked beans and rolling around in them while singing—like, the whole thing is ridiculous. But it had such a cult following. Same thing with *Rocky Horror*. I knew that if I could get it in front of the right people, that I would also most likely garner the same type of reaction that I had to watching *Rocky* and *Tommy*."

One of those people, and one who would become one of *Repo*'s most vocal advocates, was Dan Walker. He was invited to that disastrous test screening—he was, of course, one of the 8% who rated the film favorably—and recalled, "I watched it, and pretty much my life changed at that moment. Because from that point on, *Repo* was everything. I didn't know it was gonna become my job and a 24/7 thing, but that's what happened. It's like, that movie was so important, so fast. I had to be a part of it. I was writing for *Bloody Disgusting* at the time, and I thought, how do I promote this as much as I can? Because I'm excited about it, and I want horror fans to know how good it is."

Prerelease

Bousman must have been persuasive because LGF didn't toss *Repo* into the DVD dumpster. After premiering to an enthusiastic crowd at the Fantasia Film Festival in July 2008, the movie got a limited release on November 7. It went to eight screens in five US cities (Austin, New York, Los Angeles, Las Vegas, and San Francisco), where it grossed $53,684 over its first few days. Not a great return on investment for LGF's $8.5 million, but *Repo* was just getting started.

For one thing, the cosplay aspect was already in full force before the movie was even released (it played in a few festivals and at San Diego Comic-Con). At the time, Hilton said, "There are so many movies out right now which are the same thing. You know what's going to happen in the end, all the same storylines with different actors... but this movie is so unique and so different that we're already having screenings where people are coming dressed as the characters. They know all the words to the songs. It's already got a cult following, and it's not even in theaters yet. It's an experience. It's something you have to see on the big screen [because] it's an event."

Comic-Con helped bring a lot of geeky fan attention to *Repo*. Burket was there, along with her cohorts, passing out flyers and inviting likely candidates to the screening. She was the "boots on the ground" faction, so to speak, decked out in her full Henchgirl regalia. "I was there as a Henchy, and we had a couple of Genterns and Amber Sweet's boy toys walking around. I got to tell people my firsthand experiences of filming with the cast and all that, and I think it did help to keep the energy going around *Repo* that weekend. I remember the last day I was doing it; a lot of people had already heard about *Repo* and were super-excited to see it, and they already knew my character. The screening was fun! People came dressed as their favorite characters, as you do during Comic-Con, but that was probably one of the first times we started seeing that kind of fandom, and it was exciting! We truly felt like the film was connecting with and inspiring people."

While the cast and crew poured the proverbial blood, sweat, and tears into the mix and respected their film, they didn't take the whole thing too seriously. Bousman said at a press conference, "You have to know it's okay to laugh. [We] have to tell the audience that it's okay to laugh right at the very beginning of the movie because otherwise, it's going to be uncomfortable. We want them laughing with us, not at us. One of the first images we see of Grave Robber is when he's bashing down a wall using a human body, and you can't just help but laugh. However, *Repo* is a much more serious film than, say, *Rocky Horror*, which was all camp. I would say that our film is equal parts camp, drama, tragedy, and horror."

Reviews

No matter how encouraging those small screenings were, it did little to negate the disappointment the creative team and actors felt when seeing the major mainstream reviews, which were mostly abysmal. "Somebody dropped the ball and sent screeners to the press, including *Rolling Stone*, *The New York Times*, and *Los Angeles Times,* before any of the FX were done, and there was a missing scene, so it's (maybe) understandable that the critics didn't know what the fuck was going on in the film, and in their ignorance, they hated it," conjectured Smith.

"The idea of the director of *Saw II*, *III,* and *IV* going at Paris Hilton seems like just revenge for her punishable assaults on acting. In this atonal, faux-arty rock opera about a futuristic bull market in internal organs, Hilton is suitably clueless as Amber Sweet, the daughter of an aria-singing mob boss (Paul Sorvino). Amber trades in her organs like fashion accessories. But a new pancreas costs money. Don't pay, and the Repo Man will tear out your guts. It gets worse, much worse. Talented actors are involved, and I will spare them by not citing their names. 'Happiness is a warm scalpel,' sings Hilton. Misery is enduring this Rocky Horror Paris Show."

—Peter Travers / ***Rolling Stone***

"*Repo*! *The Genetic Opera* is easily one of the worst movies of the year, if not all time."

—Christy Lemire / ***Associated Press***

"I hated this movie."

—Ben Mankiewicz / ***At the Movies***

"I don't know if words can describe just how awful and disgusting and insulting this movie was to watch."

—Ben Lyons / ***At the Movies***

"The film is bad—not good-bad, tacky-bad, or fun-bad, just plain awful and nearly unwatchable."

—Mark Olsen / ***Los Angeles Times***

"Darren Lynn Bousman, the director of several *Saw* sequels, has devised an excruciating new torture with *Repo! The Genetic Opera*."

—Nathan Lee / ***The New York Times***

"*Repo* might have been an *SNL* or *MADtv* skit, but as a movie, it should be repossessed by its financiers."

—Claudia Puig / ***USA Today***

"If steampunk bloodbaths aren't for you, it's a long wait for the fat lady to sing."

—Sean Howe / ***Entertainment Weekly***

"This would-be cult film is unlikely to inspire *Rocky Horror*-like devotion."

—Frank Scheck / ***Hollywood Reporter***

✖✖✖

The following year, *Repo* received a Razzie. Every year since 1980, the Saturday before the Oscars, the Golden Raspberry Awards honor the year's crappiest films, and for 2008, they "honored" Hilton with not one but two awards. One was for *Repo*, and the other was for *The Hottie & the Nottie*. She did not appear in person to accept her "awards."

There was an upside and a downside to casting Hilton, Smith noted. The celebutant brought eyeballs to the movie, but "*Rolling Stone*, when Peter Travers gave his review of *Repo*, basically just said, 'Paris Hilton sucks. Again.' And that was it. He really couldn't see anything past that. As far as critics are concerned, we kind of knew we were doing something that's not classifiable. You get a better review if it's another Katy Perry record because it may be fluff, but they know it. And they can say it's as good fluff as the last fluff she did. You see the most positive reviews about mainstream pop music because the expectation is so low. Then when you get something like *Repo*, and when you can't wrap your head around it, the first thing you want to say is it sucks. You don't want to say, I didn't understand it. That was part of our job, too—to get people to understand it."

Fortunately, the niche genre and horror publications did understand *Repo*. That's where most of its positive reviews came from. When reading them (especially in their entirety), one sees that the genre journalists were far more learned regarding film and music than the bigger-name mainstream critics.

"Mayhem set to music is nothing new in films, even this millennia. Tim Burton's *Sweeny Todd* reminded viewers how unsafe it was to wade back into the barber's chair (at least during 19th Century England), but what *Repo* brings to the table is more daring and varied still: a four-color comic panel punctuated, Russo-Coenobium inspired, darkly futuristic, biological butcher-block ballyhoo set to a *Jesus Christ Superstar* beat, except the part of Judas now be played by a respectable fatherly doctor-cum-psycho killer. (Just listen to Anthony Stewart Head sing 'Legal Assassin,' and how can you not think of

'Heaven on their Minds'?) *Repo! The Genetic Opera* is a tale of routed spinal cords set to rousing musical chords. This splatter porn rock opera in *flay* minor is sharp, incisive, and bloody good fun."

—Keith Olexa / ***Horror.com***

"It's like *The Rocky Horror Picture Show* crashed head-on into the old EC horror comics of yesteryear. In a word, it is spectacular."

—Steve Barton / ***Dead Central***

"*Repo! The Genetic Opera* is indeed wild and crazy and over-the-top, but all the elements are cleverly contained. As you get swept up in the precarious premise, you may not notice that there's some real filmmaking going on. It's especially evident in an early scene involving Shilo as she sings about being 'infected' by her genetics. It's emotionally engaging, augmented by gorgeous, smooth camera sweeps and inspired editing that helps each expression resonate. When all the characters converge during a big number called 'At the Opera Tonight,' the editing talents of Harvey Rosenstock once again arouse awe. *Repo* not only sounds good, thanks to its incredible songs written by Darren Smith and Terrance Zdunich, but it also looks amazing under DP Joseph White's primary-colored gaze."

—Staci Layne Wilson / ***SYFY Wire***

✖✖✖

One of the most influential critics at the time, Leonard Maltin, did not see *Repo* until after its debut. "Months later, after the film was released, Leonard Maltin did a little thing online saying, *Repo* is good, original, and deserves a second look," said Smith. "Terrance ran into him maybe a few weeks after that and thanked him."

The Fans

The groundswell of fans emerged early. In many ways, *Repo* was a cult hit before it was even released. Fans were getting tattoos, creating elaborate cosplay clothing, and buying the soundtrack to learn all the songs.

Bishara, who'd overseen the music production prior to the film production, said he didn't foresee that the fandom would take hold to the extent it eventually did. "It was really hard to see where it would be going, and I had no idea of how it would be taken outside of a small cult audience. The first screening I was taken to was with Darren Bousman at Fantastic Fest [the largest genre film festival in the US]. It was before there was a trailer, before there was anything. Yet, people were showing up dressed up as characters from the movie, which was [eye-opening]. People were really taking to it."

Mark Burg, one of the Twisted Pictures producer principals, expressed his belief in *Repo* at a 2008 event, calling it "a one-of-a-kind movie that only comes around once every twenty years or so. It's built a true, loyal following that responds to it—either overwhelmingly positive or negative. There is nothing in between with this movie! So, I'm glad we produced it, I'm glad we financed it, and I'm glad Darren finally got to make his dream project. It's hard to project whether it'll be another *Rocky Horror*, but I hope so. If it is, I'll be here twenty years from now."

Smith recalled the excitement surrounding *Repo* when it started screening and was officially released in those few theaters. "There's nothing like the experience of seeing your name up there, literally on a marquee, at Edwards Cinema: *Repo! The Genetic Opera* by Darren Smith, Terrance Zdunich, and Darren Lynn Bousman. And people were coming up to us with all sorts of tattoos for our opening in Los Angeles and Las Vegas at Planet Hollywood. That was huge. I saw a long line, and I was like, I hope whoever's here is going to let our crowd in, but no! That *is* our crowd."

"I wish LGF had put a little more effort into it," Walker said, "because people were getting tattoos fast. It's not often that happens, except for the big-five slashers—Michael, Freddy, Jason, Ghostface, Leatherface. So the fact that people were getting *Repo* tattoos, that's when the studio should have stepped up and changed course. Even though we were packing 300 to 500 people—in costume, dressed up—in theaters every single night, LGF just didn't care. And that's where it was a little bit disheartening because they could have noticed that there was more going on here. The truth is they still didn't know what to do with it."

Still, Walker was philosophical about it and added, "If LGF had stood behind the film and if it had been shoved down everyone's throat in a major marketing way, I doubt it would have become a cult phenomenon. I think social media coming of age at the same time as LGF turning its back and the movie itself being so unique—that's what made it happen the way it did. Communities and the Repo Army wouldn't have formed, some families wouldn't even be together, and we would not be sitting here talking about this movie thirteen years later. I still love it. This is the longest I've gone not seeing it in a theater, and that's because of COVID-19."

Chela Johnson, LGF's Vice President of Marketing, did try her best to get the word out. "I wouldn't say that the studio didn't care about *Repo*. For one, I was at the studio, and I cared about it. Anything that costs money or has the potential to make money is something a studio cares about! But I would say Darren's creative and out-of-the-box approach was unique and new—very entrepreneurial—and that is not always something studios are used to or have an easy time accommodating, due to several logistical or legal reasons," she explained. "Darren was able to connect with the fans in a personal way that was not the norm back then."

Johnson was candid about the difficulty of marketing *Repo*. "Definitely a challenge. Part of that was being a musical in itself. Usually, with musicals, either you love'em, or you hate'em. Traditional musicals are aimed at a certain demo audience—they are renowned with known composers, and they usually gain popularity on Broadway for years before hitting the silver screen. This was not like making a movie adaptation of *Cats* or

Hamilton. *Repo* went the opposite way, starting at a point where nobody knew about it, and there was a learning curve."

Moreover, she said the music didn't adhere to the traditional Broadway style. "It was taking actors that were not known for singing (Bill Moseley, Paul Sorvino, Anthony Head) and putting them in singing roles. It was taking singers (Nivek Ogre, Sarah Brightman) and putting them in acting roles. It was taking a horror director and putting him with a musical. It was taking a person who at the time was quite controversial in the tabloids and not known for serious acting, much less singing (Paris Hilton), and asking people to take her seriously as an actor and a singer. It turned everything on its head. It's a Venn diagram that intersects with a very distinct and smaller group."

Benjamin Marsh, who would later go on to work as an assistant to Bousman, said, "I was in love with *Repo* right away. I knew from the second I saw the trailer that this was going to be my favorite movie. I knew the entire soundtrack before I even went to the screening. And it was amazing because everybody else in the audience did as well. So even though it was the first public showing ever, everybody was already singing along with it. To be in a theater filled with 500 people who knew the lyrics just like you did, who were already mega fans of the movie just based on the trailer, I have to say—it was the best movie-going experience I've ever had." Marsh said that the themes of *Repo* resonated with a lot of different kinds of people, but usually within the ranks of rebels and geeks.

Even though it didn't feel like it at the time, LGF's lack of interest—except for those few kindred spirits working in the publicity marketing department—was a blessing and put *Repo* in the underdog category. Everybody loves an underdog. Over ten years after *Repo*'s release, Bousman noted that the audience took real ownership of the movie. "I think one of the main reasons that the film had success was no one marketing the film and telling them it was cool. So often you look at promotions for movies with billboards and bus stop ads and radio spots and TV commercials saying, 'This is cool, this is cool.' We didn't have that.

"We basically had, at that time, MySpace. That was all that we had. I had a very small audience on MySpace. But it was through viral postings that fans saw it, and then we used the fan base to help us. We flat out asked them—listen, help us. Tell people we are coming to your town. Here are assets you can use. And the Repo Army was formed. They were the marketing machine. They felt ownership because they *were* owners of it at that point. They became the mouthpieces for what this thing would become. The more time and creativity you spend on something, the more you own it. And here are these fans, some of them high school kids, some younger, that were doing art and making videos, and to them, it was theirs because they created it. And they made friends. I think that is one of the most important aspects: they made friends and would travel from city to city to city, following us and following the show. It was a moment in time—it wasn't necessarily about the movie, my direction, the acting, the writing, the music. I think it was the fans and the community that made it what it was. And most films don't have that. Most times, you have a P&A budget, and it's the studio telling you what to think. This wasn't that. It was the fans themselves owning what we would become."

Walker agreed that there was something special and different about the era in which *Repo* was released. "There was this sort of beautiful moment in horror where all the website editors, writers, and readers knew each other. We were all friends, and in many cases, we were friends with the filmmakers and actors because we all loved the same thing. We were in the middle of this beautiful time for independent horror movies. Then everything kind of got fractured—the internet changed and became Twitter, so everybody had voices [not just the people invested]."

Walker recalled a time of true camaraderie. Everyone would participate when a new indie horror film came out. "We just wanted to champion it. It didn't matter whose it was. Oh, you've got a new movie?! Great, you're one of us. Let's find the good things about it and talk about it. And what's happening now is, it's become 'I'm right, you're wrong, you're an idiot—that is my review, and now you have to listen to my opinion because I am important and because I have 20,000 followers.' And it's not at all the same, where we [journalists] could go to a shitty movie at Shriekfest or Screamfest [two popular genre festivals in Los Angeles] and still write something nice about it. We might say, 'It's not my cup of tea, but holy shit, this one actor really stood out, or the music was fantastic, or the gore in this one was so good.' There was always something positive to find. And I feel that's kind of gone away now."

Even though *Repo* was hard to market, Johnson said it was fun. "A film like that screams for fun merch, which Darren and the other filmmakers were good at thinking up. Above all, the most fun came from having such a supportive and enthusiastic cast and filmmaking team. I had never been part of a film that had such drive and determination from *all* cast members to make it a success. Every single person involved cared about the project. Every person was willing to give of themselves to help make it work. They each had their own following and their own fan base demo, from Paris Hilton to Skinny Puppy to traditional film fans. That is rare, and that made it special."

Tim Meunier, an events coordinator who would head one of the most beloved and longest-lived *Repo* shadow casts, Amber's Sweets, admitted that he hated the movie the first time he saw it. "I had no idea what it was when I rented it off Blockbuster. No idea it was a musical, even. I clearly didn't do any research other than reading the headlines and seeing who the stars were. I saw Paris Hilton was in it and thought that was interesting. I played it, and about two songs in, I decided I hated it. So, I was on my Blu-ray controller, trying to eject the movie out of the player, but it wouldn't. The player was protesting and saying, 'No, you're going to keep watching this movie.' It never did that before. Never did it after. Renting a Blu-ray from Blockbuster was seven bucks, and I figured I might as well get my money's worth. Then "Legal Assassin" with Anthony Stewart Head started, and I couldn't keep my eyes off the screen. I was just completely enthralled. Probably the first time I ever experienced goosebumps when I watched a movie was during the "Chase the Morning" scene. I played the whole film three times in a row that day."

Burket recalled, "It created such a strong reaction with people. They either loved it or despised it... nothing in between. It's not a show that will leave you guessing how you feel! To me, that's good art."

Like so many fans, Meunier fell in love with rock musicals and began to seek them out and broaden his horizons. He hadn't even seen *The Rocky Horror Picture Show* before discovering *Repo*. "And now I love *Rocky*. I hadn't been familiar with the popular Broadway stuff either, but now I am. Because of *Repo*, which was a gateway, I'm into musicals and live theater."

Who's a typical fan of *Repo*? They were usually young, but not always. They were usually into musical theater, but not always. They were usually cosplayers, but not always. They were usually women, goths, or gay men, but not always. Pretty much impossible to pinpoint, but there are some pervading theories and informed opinions.

"They are disenfranchised; they're people that embrace the absurd and weird," Bousman asserted. "I think that one of the things that made *Rocky* so exciting to witness and be a part of both in theatrical settings and stage settings was it basically embraced being weird. They created a place where you could dress up in fishnet pantyhose two sizes too small and paint your face with the most ridiculous makeup and still be embraced and welcomed. Most films don't do that. I think that with *Repo*, we were so flamboyant and over-the-top, we embraced 'be who you want to be.' Do whatever you want to do, and we'll still accept you."

Chelsi Scovern runs an Instagram account devoted to *Repo*. "I first saw it in 2008. I was a goth, barely fourteen, and loved the aesthetic of a darker world. I could relate to a rebellious girl who was handed a bag of shit and just wanted to live freely and follow her heart. My first impression was that it was a big fuck you to societal standards. "It" girl Paris Hilton and Nickelodeon star Alexa PenaVega gone goth—it seemed like a rebellious move, and it looked like they enjoyed every scene. I just thought it was cool. The obsession did not start until I was older when I could understand the deeper meaning. Each character was trying to fill their void only to bury themselves deeper. So much truth in that far-fetched world."

There was an outsider aesthetic to *Repo*, Walker noted, that spoke to the fans who considered themselves different or not part of the widely accepted norm. Some people connected with Shilo, a teenager hidden from society and rebelling against her dad. "And then there's her blood disease," he said. "For every fan who had health ailments, there was a character they could

BEHIND THE SCENES

Legal Assassin
Scene 4
Intro
DDL loop
Bowed guitar
oh— (assassin)
Eb
N.P.
lie.

Model Citizen

BROUGHT TO YOU BY YOUR

POSTERS

FROM THE PRODUCERS OF SAW
ALEXA VEGA
ANTHONY STEWART HEAD
SARAH BRIGHTMAN
PARIS HILTON
OGRE
TERRANCE ZDUNICH
with BILL MOSELEY
and
PAUL SORVINO
REPO!
"AN INSTANT CULT CLASSIC" - Joseph McCabe, FEARnet.com

Soundtrack poster.

Japanese poster.

PREMIERES

Las Vegas Theatrical
Premiere / 2008

A FILM BY

Soundtrack Listening Party / 2008.

Conventions + Fans

San Diego Comic Con / 2008.

KOSHER MARKET

relate to. Also, the *Repo* world encouraged all body types. Everybody wasn't perfect, from the extras to the actual actors. You know, Sarah Brightman was an older lady, a little bit curvy and not the skin-and-bones waif. But there is Paris Hilton, a young, skin-and-bones waif right next to her. You didn't have to be a supermodel like what's popular now. If a new superhero movie is coming out, you can bet those actors are in the gym 24/7. Not many moviegoers can relate to that."

Once the very short initial run was over, fans were still hungry for the *Repo* experience. Just renting the Blu-ray wasn't going to cut it—so Bousman came up with a truly inventive, audacious plan.

CHAPTER 7

ROADSHOW

"Hey, let's put on a show!" It's an old Hollywood trope, popularized by black and white musicals, usually starring Mickey Rooney and Judy Garland. But Bousman made it a reality in 2007 by taking film prints of *Repo* to various movie theaters across the country—historic, revival-type establishments—and creating an event. These included shadow casts, costume contests, live performances, Q&As, and face time with the filmmakers and actors. Oh, and they played the movie, too!

A few months before its release, *Repo* played at the prestigious Fantasia Film Festival in Montreal, Canada, where it won the Fantasia Ground-Breaker Award. The film was also nominated for Audience Favorite at the Toronto After Dark Film Festival and played to great enthusiasm at Fantastic Fest in Austin, Texas.

Despite the groundswell of enthusiasm from fans and critics at Fantasia in Montreal and Fantastic Fest in Austin (prize wins, sold-out shows, ticket scalping, and moviegoers dressed up as the film's characters), LGF was steadfastly sticking to their limited release plan. So Bousman decided to put a seven-city tour together on his own. The maverick director paid his way and carried the print with him on airplanes to Portland, Seattle, Chicago, Kansas City, Pittsburgh, Orlando, and Atlanta through November 10-17 of that year.

"I refused to accept LGF playing the going-straight-to-video card. I just wouldn't accept it. And I got together with the creators and some of the producers and said, 'let's put our money where our mouth is.' I went into the LGF offices and said 'give me the film back. You guys take video, take the whole movie market, but give me the theatrical prints. Let me try.' They agreed, and the roadshow was born. We all wish *Repo* was a huge hit, so we wouldn't have to do that. We all hoped it would be put on 3,000 screens and be the next *Chicago*. But that wasn't in the cards. So, we had to do a quick pivot and try something else."

While Walker is critical of LGF's handling of *Repo*'s release and marketing plan, he admitted, "I don't think they were wrong in saying, 'We don't know what to do with this, so we're gonna look the other way. Let Darren do his roadshow, and we'll throw it to the wolves and see what happens.' And that's where it got interesting." The initial roadshow, thanks to the filmmakers' determination and popular demand, just kept on going.

Bishara agreed that the roadshow idea was a great way to cater to niche fans. "There is a history of movies going on the road that really nailed them down. Bob Shea (of New Line Cinema) would take *Pink Flamingos* around, and other John Waters films, [so] Darren was tapping into this barker mentality, but it was not false. It's so extremely genuine that he has this complete commitment to his enthusiasm."

Walker toured the country along with Bousman, and whoever else was along for different parts of the ride, doing everything from coordinating rental cars to filming the events for a documentary. He accumulated 400 hours of footage and plans on turning it into a retrospective documentary.

"I think Kevin Smith started touring his movies right around the end of our *Repo* tour, but we were able to do this thing that no other independent films were doing at the time," Walker said. He recalled that many of the local Los Angeles genre film directors were picking Bousman's brain on how he managed to pull off the feat. Many recognized the cinematic landscape was changing. "You couldn't just put a movie out anymore and give it time for an audience to find it. You had to get in a bus and peddle, just like an old-timey carnival barker. You had to put a little more into making it a show than just, 'here's a movie.' Because if it's just another film, it's a catalog piece after a few months, and it fades away."

The roadshows truly brought people together, Walker recalled. "I remember seeing a couple of engagements, and I can think of at least four couples still together to this day that met through *Repo*—with kids and everything, more than ten years later. It did get a little bit wild," he added and laughed. "Like a theater company, where everybody in the cast is banging another castmate. But that's par for the course in the world of actors!"

"You could write an entire book about the shenanigans that took place on the roadshows," Bousman said. "We probably should have been thrown in jail numerous times! But I think one of the greatest parts of the roadshow was the camaraderie. I go to the premiere of any other film of mine, and I stand in front of the theater, and I wave and say thank you, and I might sign an autograph as I'm running out to a bar to get completely hammered, but the difference with *Repo* is we were with the fans every step of the way. We would go to dinner with them. We would go drinking with them after the screening. Have breakfast with them in the morning. And the fans literally became an army. Hence the birth of the Repo Army. Some of these people I still talk to, to this day. Thirteen years later, I still talk to them. These fans have supported me throughout my career. It all started with *Repo*. I can't think of another movie where something like that would have happened."

Although LaRose had a small part in the film, he also got swept up Bashara in the road trip whirlwind, to a point. "I caught up on some of the tour and a couple of stops. I don't have the energy for the whole thing like they did. I mean, it is just exhausting to think about! I saw the whole *Rocky Horror* kind of vibe, which is what I think they were hoping this would turn into. That passionate kind of kitschy little thing where people dress up and participate and do the whole shadow cast thing. Before *Repo*, I had never seen a shadow cast—I had never heard of such a thing—and it was a blast to see these groups of people being so passionate about something. And to talk to them after the show, to be able to answer their questions, it was great. That's part of why I like being in this business; to see the response from fans."

Walker asserts that the response from fans for *Repo* was always positive. "Calling the characters assholes like they do at *Rocky* screenings... didn't happen with *Repo*. *Rocky Horror* fans can be pretty harsh." In fact, according to Walker, early on, when *Repo* started playing midnight revival theaters, some *Rocky* fans saw *Repo* as competition. "We all love *Rocky*," said Walker of himself and the Repo Army, "and about two-thirds of the *Rocky* community was like, it's not *Rocky*, but it's cool. But a lot of them were like, this movie is shit, and we don't like it. We don't want anything to do with it because they're trying to be *Rocky,* and they're trying too hard to be a cult film, and you can't be a cult film. You have to earn it."

Moseley attended many *Repo* roadshows, plus events at various horror and film conventions. "I've seen, probably, close to a dozen *Repo* cosplay shows over the years. Mostly at conventions. And it's a big deal. I consider it an honor to be invited, and usually, they just want me to say something before the movie, but I like to stay. I like to stay and watch. Because the movie is so cool, but also, to show respect to the people who are making the effort to do the *Repo* shadow cast."

Walker said, "Bill Moseley was always an important guest because he has the horror legacy. And all the people that were there for Moseley were there for Bousman as well, because of the *Saw* films. But if Alexa was there, there would be a bunch of fans of hers from *Spy Kids* or *Sleepover*. It was really fascinating to see all these walks of life come together for a weird musical."

About a year after beginning the road shows, Bousman felt vindicated. At the time, he said, "It proved to us that we were not out of our minds after so many bad reviews, so many people saying the movie was horrific and the worst movie of the year, and all these other things." He had begun to wonder. "We basically got torn apart by the mainstream. You start to second-guess, like, maybe this is bad, maybe people don't like it. And then we went on the road tours, and we were selling out theaters way in advance. We'd show up, and there'd be lines wrapping around blocks. It was like we were rock stars. The fans were screaming. We'd get out of the car, and everyone knew who we were. We were getting swarmed by fans, and we'd stay every night after every show to sign every autograph. We'd get to talk to the fans, and that never happened with *Saw*. I was never attacked. People never waited in lines. People never came dressed up for *Saw*. The roadshows for this movie were validation of why we were doing what we were doing."

Bousman is convinced that if he had just accepted the straight-to-DVD tag and moved on to his next project, the movie would have died. "Myself, Terrance, Joe Bishara, Darren Smith... we wouldn't let this thing die because it is an important movie. Open up the newspaper," he said in 2008, "and look at every movie that's out right now. Ninety percent are remakes, sequels, or things that we've seen a thousand times before with different actors called something new. *Repo* is why I got into moviemaking and hopefully why people go to the movies—to see something they haven't experienced before. Originality is not dead; it's just not rewarded."

Final Big Screen Bows

I was on hand for *Repo*'s final big screen bow on January 24, 2009, in West Los Angeles. That screening capped off the third nationwide road tour, and the bash was huge. I was there on opening night in Hollywood on November 7, 2008, and while the theater was sold-out and there were a few people in costumes, there wasn't a lot of singing along and no shadow casting. The *Repo*mania all came later and gained momentum when the guys went on the road showing the movie across the nation. That initial tour justified two more and several one-off revivals screenings over the next decade.

I wrote in my report for *SYFY WIRE* at the time, "I've been to a lot of cult movie events. I've seen some of the true gems, along with singing and bopping and playfully heckling audiences—*Rocky Horror*, *The Song Remains the Same*, *The Apple*, and

Phantom of the Paradise, to name a few of the heavyweights with steadfast fandom. But nothing could quite prepare me for this outpouring of love, devotion, and support. More than six hundred fans filled the historic Laemmle Royal Theater, nearly every one of them dressed as favorite characters: Blind Mag, Pavi, Repo Man, Genterns, and Henchgirls, Amber Sweet, et al. Many of them drove and flew across the country just to see their favorite flick off in style. On hand for the farewell gala were Bousman, Smith, Zdunich, producer Mark Burg, music producer Bishara, singer Nancy Long, and actors from the film including Ogre, Moseley, PenaVega, and Hilton."

Ogre was a latecomer to the roadshow mania, making his first appearance at the last show. "This is my first road tour stop. I was supposed to go to one along the way before this, but I went underground for a while and started working on the next Skinny Puppy record. This is amazing, though. I've seen people dressed up for my concerts, but I've never seen anything like this for a movie. I think Darren's done a slam dunk job on this. At first, a lot of people were confused at how to respond to this movie but now look at them. I'm shocked by some of the makeups, too—I mean, there are some better Pavi's than me! It's a really good thing all around. I think I've gotten some new fans for my music through *Repo*, who might not otherwise have heard it. It's hard to tell with my solo tour [which just wrapped], but I've definitely seen an increase on the Skinny Puppy boards, and we'll see what happens with this upcoming record, if that reaps the *Repo*s!"

Burket recalled another significant event that occurred a couple of years after *Repo*'s release. "I remember getting to be a part of the Sacramento Horror Film Festival in 2009. *Repo* was a featured film on their horror film slate, and the local shadow cast troupe, (Tim Meunier's) Amber's Sweets, performed some scenes alongside the film when they screened it." It was Amber Sweet's debut public performance. "It was so awesome! They were great. Tim flew us there, and I got to reunite with my Henchy counterpart, and we met with fans and signed photos, programs, boobs, and other body parts... it was just so much fun. To look someone in the eyes and listen to them while they tell you how something you were a part of deeply changed their lives for the better or helped them through a rough time or just made them happy... it was both energizing and beautifully humbling. It felt so wonderful to know that all the blood, sweat, and tears that went into the making of that film did what it was supposed to do—spread love! I know that sounds so damn cheesy, but honestly, at the end of the day, I just wanted people to feel the same love for the film that myself and everyone I worked with on it throughout the years felt for it. And to learn of the friendships and relationships that grew from fans meeting each other... there's nothing like it. It's so special when something like that happens."

CHAPTER 8
LEGACY

"I've gone to the amusement park and ridden the best ride first. What that has done is educate me," Bousman said in 2008. "I learned more about moviemaking and politicking from *Repo* than any film school I've been to. I've learned that there's a very conventional approach that everyone takes in their life. This goes outside of filmmaking, too. You do this: you go from point A to point B to point C to point D, and hopefully, by the end of your life, point X-Y-Z. And in trying to go around that, you're considered weird. People say you can't do that, and it's wrong. Even my agents and manager said, 'You can't do this. It's not done.' With *Repo,* I went around the system. It was completely unconventional every step of the way, and I proved that you don't have to follow this conventional path. You can still get to the same point. I think that if you're a filmmaker, you should be passionate about what you are doing. And part of being a filmmaker is bringing a vision, your vision, to the screen. I'll do that with every movie that I do. I will fight and I will fight and I will fight until the vision is on the screen."

Bousman continued (in 2008), "I think that we're gonna be able to tell in ten years, fifteen years, what *Repo* actually did. I know it sounds really cocky or arrogant, but I really believe this. Years from now, they're going to think of *Repo* in a much different light. I'm not saying it's going to be a financial success, and I'm not saying it's going to change the world of filmmaking, but we are setting forth on a course of action that will change the way people think about independent movies."

After several years of perspective, Bousman reflected on how *Repo* might have affected his career. "Well, I'll tell you, I probably would have a lot more money and a lot bigger films. *Repo* derailed my string of number one hits. I had three movies open at number one, and I could have, at that point, made any film within a reasonable budget that I wanted to, coming off the success of *Saw II*. *Repo* was a colossal failure, and I became untouchable for many years, [stuck] in director's jail. That is all due to the perception of the failure of *Repo*. Because the reality is *Deadline Hollywood*, *Hollywood Reporter*, *Variety*—they don't care that we gained a cult fandom. What they care about is, did the movie make money? By the time the movie made its money back, it was too late. That story, for them, had already been written.

"It definitely hurt me, but from another perspective, it showed me that I could do whatever I wanted. I wasn't ever going to let someone tell me that what I'd made had no audience for it. It pushed me to just continue to make my passion projects.

So, I've had a lot of hits and misses, but the point is, they're all things that I wanted to do. From *Repo* to *Devil's Carnival* to going overseas and making a Japanese TV series to creating immersive theater—these are all things that I set out to do. If I had not made *Repo,* I would have been a lot safer in my career, and I probably would have a much bigger house, but I don't think I would have been as happy. I am proud of the weirdness I've put out there."

While *Repo* was quickly forgotten by most of the mainstream, the underground press and fan base kept it alive and evolving. For instance, many shadow casts formed during the road tours continued. Meunier's Amber's Sweets was one of the better-known of these troupes. "You get a bunch of horror fans together, and suddenly, you've made a new friend, and you start talking about the films. It's a lot of fellowship, a lot of camaraderie, a lot of bonding. It's a very "Island of Misfit Toys" family experience, so to speak. You know, it's just like theater. Theater has that same vibe, except a lot of these shadow casters never did theater. They were either cosplayers or just sitting idly by watching movies, and then they thought, hey, this sounds like something I can get into. So, it was a bit more accessible, a bit more amateur. A lot of these performers I started out with in Amber's Sweets have gone on to act in films, joined burlesque troops, become drag kings or queens, and are very notable in their community. It's really cool to see where they've gone, from introductory shadow casting to engaging in their performance art careers."

For one fan, his love of *Repo* paved his way into the film business. It all started with seeing the trailer online, then meeting Bousman. Marsh recalled that when he was in high school in 2008, he was dealing with a severe case of OCD, and one of the only things that calmed his nerves was watching horror movies. He watched Bousman's *Saw* movies, then found out about his favorite director's upcoming film, which was, of course, *Repo*.

"My particular OCD wasn't anything to do with germs; it was with my body image," Marsh said. This meant he was loath to leave his home. "One day, my dad convinced me to go out." They went to Marsh's favorite arthouse movie theater. "I loved going to this theater, so my dad was online looking at showtimes. We pulled up their website, and their entire front page was this advertisement for a special screening for this new movie, *Repo*, directed by Darren Bousman, who had done *Saws II*, *III,* and *IV*. There was even a Q&A and a meet and greet. I'm like, oh my god! This is my chance to meet my idol. And when I found out what *Repo* was about and everything, I thought, 'this is literally everything I want in a movie.' I was so nonfunctional with my OCD at the time that I wasn't going to school, and my dad was just like, if you get your ass back to school, I'll buy you the *Repo* screening tickets. I was at school the next day. That's literally what helped me get my life back on track."

Once Marsh had tickets in hand for the *Repo* screening, "I immediately contacted Darren on social media and told him how I was a big fan of his work with the *Saw* series, and how I was super-excited that he created *Repo* and was having this special screening in my hometown of Cincinnati. He accepted my friend request. Writes me back. And he tells me, 'Hey man, so sorry you're dealing with this. I dealt with OCD when I was in high school. If I can get through it, you can get through it too.' Those words from my idol are exactly what I needed to hear at that point in my life because I was at the lowest of the low. Hearing that from somebody well-known and somebody that inspired me literally saved my life. He also said, 'Hey, dude, I can't wait to meet you at the screening. I'll see you there.'"

Marsh dressed for the screening in a suit and tie—the works—but soon saw that the rest of the audience were in full cosplay mode. He stood out. "This is literally my favorite story to tell," Marsh said with a chuckle. "There were maybe 400-500 of us waiting in the lobby for Darren and Terrance and the rest of the *Repo* crew to show up. And I kid you not, when Darren arrives, he literally makes his way through the entire crowd of people, ignores everybody else, sees me, and heads straight for me, and he just gives me the biggest hug."

After the screening, Marsh and his dad got to talk with Bousman. The director asked the seventeen-year-old what his career plan was, and Marsh said he wanted to go to film school, then move to Los Angeles to get into the film business. "Darren gave me his personal email address and asked me to look him up when I got to L.A." Marsh enrolled in film school in

Michigan and ran into Bousman again in 2010 at a screening for the director's remake of *Mother's Day*. Once again, Bousman encouraged Marsh to look him up in L.A.

After seeing *Repo*, Marsh became a superfan. "Being seventeen, the song 'Seventeen' resonated with me. And I've always been a fan of classic rock, so I loved the Joan Jett cameo in the movie. After I got the soundtrack, 'Seventeen' was my anthem. That was the song that was on repeat. That's probably the one that meant the most to me because I could relate to Shilo's line, 'Why, oh why, are my genetics such a bitch?!' That's kind of what it felt like. I was constantly screaming that line over and over again. But then I could also relate to Amber. She's all about trying to create the best image of herself. I felt like I was a combination of those two characters.

"Even my parents, who don't watch horror movies at all, were able to find something that they loved in *Repo*. I think a huge part of that is respect for how *Repo* changed my life. They realized that there's more to it than just the blood, guts, and gore." He added, "You know, every other fan that I met maybe didn't have the exact same story as myself with the movie, but for a lot of them, the movie saved their lives, too. Whether they suffered from depression or abuse from a relationship, so many people have been saved by this movie... and I think that doesn't get talked about enough. Maybe it's too emotional for people to talk about, but I know this movie has saved lives."

After Marsh moved out west, he got a job working as a production assistant. It was not as glamorous as he'd hoped. "I was managing sixty extras at an L.A. community college in Hollywood— the only production assistant they had, because it was a little, low-budget, indie horror flick. I was over it. The producers weren't treating me right, my expectation meter was running low, and basically, it was a nightmare. One day, I kept getting these calls from a blocked number, but I was so busy and stressed, so I would immediately hang it up. The calls kept coming. Eventually, I kind of snapped and answered it like, what the fuck do you want? Why do you keep calling me? It was Darren Bousman, saying he needed a personal assistant starting ASAP. So that's how I went from OCD-ridden fanboy to his personal assistant."

The two worked together for years, with Marsh becoming the assistant director and stage manager for Bousman's Immersive Theater Productions. While Marsh was working for Bousman, the director created another rock and roll horror musical, *The Devil's Carnival. Devil's Carnival* featured many *Repo* alums, including Zdunich, Moseley, Sorvino, PenaVega, and LaRose, to name a few. Marsh said, "After *Devil's Carnival* premiered, we took it on a road tour, and I met so many incredible fans. Obviously, *Devil's Carnival* fans are *Repo* fans by default."

Moseley agreed. "*The Devil's Carnival* really is 'Son of *Repo*' in so many ways."

Walker said he was in on the brainstorming sessions during the creation of *The Devil's Carnival.* "There's obviously an audience," he said. "What do we do? The audience wants more from us. We can only take the same movie on the road so many times. I remember Darren and Terrance had talked about doing a short." It was a proof of concept, not unlike the one made for *Repo* all those years before. "We found L.A. Circus in Riverside, CA, and once we had the location, that's when all the pieces started falling into place. The music was being written around the location, and we started casting. We knew we had to do a follow-up—we all wanted to do a follow-up. As for *Repo* itself, Lionsgate wasn't going to give up the rights or any money for us to make a sequel to a thing they didn't want in the first place. So, we went and found independent financing, and we did *The Devil's Carnival* in 2012 and a sequel in 2015. They're their own weird anomalies."

Walker changed the course of his career to take a ride on the *Repo* train. "I quit my job in horror journalism to cheer this movie on full time to as many people as would listen. I made a puppet version of the movie for the tour—I made it just for fun, but Darren and Terrance loved it so much that they took me on tour with my little puppet." This led to Walker continuing his work with *The Devil's Carnival* and Zdunich and Saal Hendelman's current endeavor, American Murder Song (live concert performances that pay homage to vintage murder ballads of the 1920s and 30s). "I just did a photo shoot for American Murder Song about two weeks ago and directed videos for Terrance. We still work together all the time. Darren Bousman and I are working on possibly putting a documentary together properly for *Repo.* It's become a thing that I can't escape even if I wanted to, but I don't want to. I love it."

Smith said that when a film reaches cult status, it is out of the creators' hands. "I'm very gratified that people want my autograph, and they treat me well when I go to these events. They have a kind of ownership interest, and it's great. It really is. I can sit back and watch this creation that started in my head, but now it's like a child. They grow up, and they're gonna be who they are. They're going to develop, and you try to do your best to help them grow, but after that, it's going to be what it is. And I think that *Repo,* in a way, is kind of like that. Honestly, I didn't think I would be talking about a movie in 2021 that was released in 2008."

To some, *cult* means "bad" in cinema fandom. Walker doesn't appreciate comparisons to other recent cult films like *The Room* (2003) and *Birdemic: Shock and Terror* (2010). "I always got mad when people compared it to [those] because they are bad movies. They're genuinely bad films, but the filmmakers don't know it. And people like them *because* they're bad films. I think *Repo*, like *Rocky*, is truly good. And they have music going for them. Fans like us have listened to the soundtracks a million times—because it's great music! Period."

One of the significant "gotchas!" was when *Rolling Stone*, six years after its initial thumbs-down of the movie, voted *Repo* one of the "25 Greatest Cult Films of All Time." *Repo* was in good company with *Hedwig and the Angry Inch*, *Pink Floyd: The Wall*, and of course, the OG cult musical, *The Rocky Horror Picture Show*.

"In terms of being a promoter for this stuff, it's like... could I ever get actors from a Scorsese film to my film fest? Can I get Tarantino himself to come to the fest? Probably not. And so, the fact that these films are a little bit more in the corner, so to speak, makes them cooler. Talking to the creators and actors has been so phenomenal," Meunier said. "To bring them out to the film shows and to have them meet fans is just amazing. To see the difference it makes in people's eyes when they are able to connect with Darren Bousman or Darren Smith or Terrance, it's just a beautiful thing. Sometimes things like that can go very wrong, you know, when you meet your heroes. But they've been just wonderful to fans. They are bar none, some of my favorite people that I've booked and worked with, and I would bring them out again and again just because of how fantastic they were with the fans. From the promoter aspect, that's just priceless."

New fans are still finding *Repo* to this day. Scovern says some people who've never seen the movie stumble onto her Instagram account and wind up following. "They check it out for the aesthetic or the love of actors like Terrance Zdunich, Paris Hilton, Ogre, or Sarah Brightman." The demographics are a mix. "Most of the fan base I find now is the younger generation who can relate to Shilo. I do think Instagram boosts the *Repo* fan base. This past year (2021), I found a lot of horror podcasters introducing the movie. Some of the reviews are not in favor, but that still attracts viewers, and true fans love to take up for the movie. In my view, you either love it or hate it. For those who love it, they love every bit. It is a dark film that helps you understand the twisted mind of an extreme surgery/drug addict, and there is a beauty in wanting something versus doing what is right. A very reckless and angry Shilo choosing the righteous path in such a dark dystopian world gives a sense of hope. It is fun introducing this unique feature to new friends and debating with those who oppose on why it's the best movie ever made."

Smith said he's still seeing new fandom as well. "It's always been great, but then we started noticing a few years back these new shadow casts that we don't know and never heard of. We had people all over the world contacting us and saying they loved it. To this day, I get emails from people who are young, like, twenty years old. They weren't around in the first iteration of *Repo*, so we're getting another generation of people. My niece, who was a student at Yale University, told me they did a whole talk and a lecture about *Repo*. So, we're getting up there in the establishment. There's a lot in there. If you watch it forty times, you're going to see subtleties on that fortieth viewing. And if you watch it fifty times, you're going to see stuff that even I didn't notice."

Bousman said, "I don't know how many people have reached out to me to either tell me their kid's name is Shilo or show me their Repo Army tattoo or a fan video they made. There's fan fiction and Deviant Art accounts devoted to *Repo*. It's a constantly changing art piece. The movie is never done because it's always being altered by the fans. And to me, that is one of the coolest, most liberating, proudest things as a filmmaker. It's funny. No one comes up to me on the street and talks about *Spiral* or *Saw*—never. But people do come up to me on *Repo* quite a bit. Just the other day, I was getting pizza kind of close to my house. I get handed the receipt, and as I get in the car, I look down and notice something handwritten in big letters. It just said, TESTIFY!—which was one of the major catchphrases from *Repo*."

In some ways, *Repo* is still a big part of Laura's life. "I feel like I am still on that roller coaster. Darren had said to me before we even started *Repo*, 'I want to make this movie. This is my passion. I will be giving up millions of dollars from the *Saw IV* paycheck to put it into *Repo*, but this is what I want to do. What do you think?' Well, we didn't have kids yet, so I said, of course! Follow your dreams! I believe in you and this project! I was really sad when it felt that the movie was not getting the support that it deserved. It's such a special film, and I still believe in it. The commercial failure was extremely difficult on Darren. He had just come off three number one movies in the world, so it was a huge blow. But the critical acclaim and rallying by fans made it more than worth the pain and heartache."

White has mostly left the feature film world and now shoots fashion and commercials. But he looks back fondly on the days of shooting *Repo* and appreciates its legacy. "It's something I'm still very proud of years later and thankful that I was a part of it. Darren had the balls to follow up the *Saw* movies with a sci-fi horror rock opera musical... it's fucking insane. I have so much respect for him, betting on himself. If he had just gone and made a bunch of other franchise sequels and other horror films, he would have been a working director, and he'd have a big house and whatever, but I think making the choices to do *Repo* and *The Devil's Carnival* and things like that contribute to his legacy as a filmmaker. I think a lot of people, in horror especially, can become these journeyman or journeywoman directors, where they just keep doing those things, never getting the big budgets, never doing something too tiny, just working. What Darren did was a pretty fucking boss move. He said this is something I'm passionate about. This is something that is interesting to me. And I've done these films that have been ridiculously commercially successful, so I'm going to leverage that to be able to do what I want."

At this writing, Zdunich has segued from acting in musicals into performing live music full time. He has a duo with Hendelman where they play old-timey characters, Mister Storm and Mister Tender, and sing their original tunes about "music, blood, and history."

Smith continues to write music and lyrics, mainly for his independent film projects. He's also the author of several short story anthologies and a book of poetry. He doesn't have any plans to revisit or revive *Repo*. "When we got *Repo* out, that was the result of seven years of work, and I wanted to do something else. The ten-minute opera, *Necomerchant's Debt*, turned into this horror-themed musical feature. But that's not my inclination to do horror. I have other genres and media that I'm more passionate about exploring right now."

As mentioned in the Introduction, Smith and I have been working on book and film projects together. Our feature film, *The Second Age of Aquarius* (based on our short story, "Fandom/Phantom"), was released in February, 2022. It has no horror elements; rather, it's a cross between *Weird Science*, Oliver Stone's *The Doors*, and *The Odd Couple*. Smith wrote several all-original, '60s period-correct rock songs for the movie and released a soundtrack.

Bousman had a megahit with his return to the *Saw* universe with his film *Spiral* in 2021. Is he still interested in doing a sequel to *Repo*? "I guess I should say never say never. I said I never would go back and make another *Saw* film, but then I did. *Repo* was one of my best experiences as a filmmaker because it's the one movie that is most true to what I set out to make. Because I was a producer on the movie and because it was such a passion for me, I retained a lot more control over *Repo* than other films. Because of that, I look at it, and I'm like, fuck, I want to go back to this world, and I want to play in that world again, and there's so much more I think I could do with it.

"When the idea was originally conceived, it was a three-part thing that we wanted to do, with *Repo* being the middle part.

There was a prequel, and then there was a sequel after that. Years after we made it, Terrance and Darren wrote a very, very detailed treatment of what the next one would be. And there were even some early recordings of music to show what we wanted it to be. But [then] *Repo* was a financial failure, and I think everyone kind of lost hope. Now it is no longer that failure—everyone has made their money back on the film at this point, and it has gone on to have such a cult following—so the only thing I can hope for is that we do what Rob Zombie did with *3 from Hell* a decade-plus after *The Devil's Rejects*. I think there is a world in which maybe we would come back, but there's a lot of red tape. It would be a very long, long, long conversation with Lionsgate. But I think all the characters would definitely come back... including some of those who died. I joked about that with Paul Sorvino and Anthony Stewart Head and Sarah Brightman, but I think every single person would come back if given the opportunity."

In my view, one of the significant things that set *Repo* apart from its cult brethren is its combination of top-notch music, striking lyrics, and disturbing, thought-provoking themes. It's not a flick you can put on in the background; *Repo* commands your concentration as you listen to the story unfold entirely through lyrics. It's a genuine opera with only a few spoken words. It is not always an easy movie to watch, and it screams for additional viewings to appreciate all its aspects fully, but the reward is great.

Many science fiction films become dystopian, self-fulfilling prophecies—but there's only one that stars Anthony Stewart Head singing, dancing, and slicing and dicing. There are movies about diminishing resources and warnings about what could happen if the human right to life becomes a commodity—but there's only one featuring Paris Hilton and Nivek Ogre trading faces like playing cards. Today we worry about class division, the wealth divide, and our inability to afford to maintain a decent quality of life and basic healthcare—and "21st Century Cure" reinforces our fears, set to a seductive rock beat and sung lustily by Terrance Zdunich.

Repo riffs on the actions of these flawed but upbeat individuals, their feelings of love and despair, their thrill-seeking and addictions. There's a child yearning to express herself and a parent's ultimate sacrifice. While the examples are extreme—and extremely gory—there are kernels of truth and relatability instilled within each and every character.

We can imagine living the world of *Repo*, which is both alarming and alluring.

ACKNOWLEDGMENTS

I want to thank everyone who was kind enough to take the time to be interviewed for this book. Your memories and perspectives were invaluable in putting together a complete picture of *Repo*.

I'd also like to thank my Beta readers—Linda Rose, Sherry Thomas, Jamie Jones, Robin Fuchs Brumfield, and Kate DeJonge—most of you had never seen *Repo* before this, and now you've righted that wrong! I'm glad I could be the one to introduce you to this unique film. Now, go forth and "testify!"

IMAGE CREDITS

All photos are from the collections of Staci Wilson, Darren Lynn Bousman, and Darren Gordon Smith. This excludes Las Vegas Theatrical Premiere photography (photo plates 10 and 11), which are courtesy WENN Rights Ltd / Alamy Stock Photo.

Repo! The Genetic Opera is © 2008 Lionsgate Films

ABOUT THE AUTHOR

Staci Layne Wilson is an L.A. native who enjoys traffic, wildfires, and earthquakes—but since her move to Las Vegas, she's learned to love 110-degree summers, drive-thru wedding chapels, and casinos that still reek of the Rat Pack's cigars. She has been a professional writer since the age of twelve when she was hired as a columnist for a national magazine. When she's not writing books, she is making movies (*Cabaret of the Dead*, *The Ventures: Stars on Guitars*, and *The Second Age of Aquarius*).

Catch up with Staci at
StaciLayneWilson.com